Jorge Amado

Twayne's World Authors Series

Latin American Literature

David W. Foster, Editor

Arizona State University

TWAS 767

Jorge Amado receiving the degree of Doctor Honoris Causa from the Université Lumière Lyon II, 1987. *Photograph by Zélia Gattai Amado reproduced courtesy of Jorge and Zélia Gattai Amado and the Fundação Casa de Jorge Amado, Salvador, Bahia.*

Jorge Amado

By Bobby J. Chamberlain

University of Pittsburgh

Twayne Publishers
A Division of G. K. Hall & Co. • Boston

PQ
9697
.A647
Z585
1990

Jorge Amado
Bobby J. Chamberlain

Copyright 1990 by G. K. Hall & Co.
All rights reserved.
Published by Twayne Publishers
A division of G. K. Hall & Co.
70 Lincoln Street
Boston, Massachusetts   02111

Copyediting supervised by Barbara Sutton.
Book production by Janet Z. Reynolds.
Book design by Barbara Anderson.
Typeset in 11/12 Garamond
by Compset, Inc., Beverly, Massachusetts

First published 1990.
10 9 8 7 6 5 4 3 2 1

Library of Congress Cataloging-in-Publication Data

Chamberlain, Bobby J.
    Jorge Amado / by Bobby J. Chamberlain.
        p.   cm.—(Twayne's world authors series ; TWAS 767) (Latin
American literature)
    Includes bibliographical references.
    ISBN 0-8057-8261-3 (alk. paper)
    1. Amado, Jorge, 1912–   —Criticism and interpretation.
I. Title.   II. Series.   III. Series: Twayne's world authors series.
Latin American literature.
PQ9697.A647Z585   1990
869.3—dc20   90-34428
                                                                         CIP

For Katherine and Bobby

Contents

About the Author

Bobby J. Chamberlain received his Ph.D. in Hispanic languages and literatures from U.C.L.A. He has twice been a Fulbright-Hays fellow in Brazil. Currently associate professor of Portuguese and Spanish at the University of Pittsburgh, he has also held appointments at Michigan State University and the University of Southern California. While at M.S.U. Chamberlain served as assistant director of the Latin American Studies Center and directed the study-abroad program in Mérida, Yucatán, Mexico.

For six years Chamberlain was the director of the American Association of Teachers of Spanish and Portuguese Task Force for the Promotion of Portuguese. He was also a member of the Executive Committee of the Luso-Brazilian Division of the Modern Language Association of America. He has published widely on Brazilian literature and language and has served on the editorial boards of both the *Revista iberoamericana* and *Chasqui*. He is the coauthor (with Ronald M. Harmon) of *A Dictionary of Informal Brazilian Portuguese* (1984) and editor of *Portuguese Language and Luso-Brazilian Literature: An Annotated Guide to Selected Reference Works* (1989).

Preface

Jorge Amado is today the most widely translated Brazilian author of all times. Over the course of his literary career, which now spans almost sixty years, he has published some thirty volumes of fiction, theater, biography, memoirs, poetry, travel literature, and children's stories, many of which have subsequently been rendered into one or more of thirty-eight foreign languages. Of his twenty-one novels, most have gone through dozens of editions in Brazil alone, and several have been made into popular motion pictures or television serial dramas.

In recent years a controversy has developed over the author's later works. Since the publication in 1958 of *Gabriela, cravo e canela* (*Gabriela, Clove and Cinnamon,* 1962) Amado has largely abandoned the hard-hitting novels of social and political criticism for which he became famous in favor of social satire. The proletarian fiction and socialist realism of his earlier phase have given way to irony, picaresque humor, and parody as vehicles for his denunciation of social ills. In the late 1950s and early 1960s most critics hailed the appearance of this new, less dogmatic style as proof of the author's greater maturity. But, particularly since the mid-1970s, some literary scholars have begun to condemn the "new Amado" for what they regard as his excessive populism, trivialization of poverty, racial and sexual stereotyping, repetition of episodes and characters, and cultivation of stale, outmoded narrative formulas. Indeed, it has become unfashionable in many Brazilian literary circles to express admiration for Amado's later fiction.

This study examines salient aspects of selected Amadian novels, giving particular emphasis to the later works. Owing to the large size of the author's total oeuvre, a book-by-book analysis is beyond the scope of this volume. Nor is there an effort to treat the writer's occasional sallies outside the realm of prose fiction; systematic studies of his theater, poetry, biography, children's literature, and the like have not yet been published and will have to wait for future Amadian critics. The emphasis on Amado's more recent works over the older ones and the specific selection of novels herein dealt with are, of course, reflections of my own personal biases as a reader and critic. But they likewise correspond in large measure to the value judgments expressed by most previous Amadian scholars, as well as coinciding felicitously with the works that are best known to the novelist's English-speaking readers.

Chapter 1 serves as an introduction inasmuch as it seeks to place the author's fiction in a biographical and bibliographic context. Chapter 2 is devoted to the early novels. In it, I chart the coordinates of Amado's social realism and attempt to trace the early development of his narrative skills. This is followed by a discussion of the two most significant books of the first phase. *Jubiabá* (1935) and *Terras do sem fim* (1943; *The Violent Land,* 1945). Chapters 3–6 focus on five works of the author's later period. Chapter 3, on *Gabriela, cravo e canela,* begins with an overview of the "new" Amadian style. This is followed by a brief examination of the novelist's use of chronicle parody and a longer analysis of his portrayal of the five female characters around whom the work is structured. Chapter 4 concentrates on the two novelettes originally published together in a 1961 volume entitled *Os velhos marinheiros* (The old sailors) and later published separately. Double perspective is treated as it applies to both *A morte e a morte de Quincas Berro D'água* (*The Two Deaths of Quincas Wateryell,* 1965) and *A completa verdade sobre as discutidas aventuras do comandante Vasco Moscoso de Aragão, capitão de longo curso* (later retitled *Os velhos marinheiros ou o capitão de longo curso; Home Is the Sailor,* 1964). There is also a discussion of *Quincas*'s irreverent burlesquing of the biblical account of Christ's Passion.

Dona Flor e seus dois maridos (1966; *Dona Flor and Her Two Husbands,* 1969) is the topic of chapter 5. I begin the chapter with an exploration of the novel's sociopolitical symbolism. The possibility of an allegory is considered. Amado's use of recipes and menus to structure the work is discussed, as are his inclusion of numerous real-life characters in *Dona Flor* and later books and his frequent recourse to supernatural characters and events, many of them of Afro-Bahian origin. Chapter 6 analyzes the use of parody and stylization of *literatura de cordel* (chapbook verse) in *Tereza Batista cansada de guerra* (1972; *Tereza Batista: Home from the Wars,* 1975), paying special attention to their effects on the characterization of the female protagonist.

The final chapter attempts to synthesize the findings of the preceding ones both in order to draw some tentative conclusions about Amado's fiction and in an effort to shed light on the controversy surrounding the novelist's later works. It has not been my purpose here to undertake a systematic ideological or semiotic analysis of the author or his novels. Nor do I claim to have put to rest the critics' dispute. What I have endeavored to do is to trace the broad contours of Amadian fiction, calling particular attention to those aspects that I believe to be frequently overlooked or misinterpreted. At the same time, I have tried to avoid the "intentional fallacy" or the implication that there is but one valid meaning to be discovered in a text. Amado's novels are, in the final analysis, often marked by irresolvable oxymorons and troubling paradoxes. Attitudes and sympathies are contradictory. The greater complexities of many of his later works are concealed by seeming naïveté. And the ideology of the text sometimes appears to undercut itself. A reevaluation of the author's novelistic output is urgently needed. It is hoped, then, that the present monograph will lay the groundwork for such a project.

Of the various sections of this volume, only two subchapters have appeared previously in substantially the same form: "Roman à Clef Characters" ("Unlocking the *Roman à Clef:* A Look at the 'In-Group' Humor of Jorge Amado," *The American Hispanist* 4, no. 28 [September 1978]: 12–16) and "Recipes, Menus and Sensual Delights" ("Gastronomic Interludes in Jorge Amado's *Dona Flor e seus dois maridos*," *Tropos* 6, no. 1 [Spring 1977]: 9–26). Unless otherwise stated, all English translations from Portuguese in the present volume are my own, even in some cases where there are other, published English renditions available. All spelling in Portuguese conforms to current orthographical conventions.

I would like to thank David William Foster, Twayne's Latin American field editor, for his patience and encouragement. Special thanks must go to my wife, Kay, without whose love and inspiration this book would have never been completed.

Bobby J. Chamberlain

University of Pittsburgh

Abbreviations Used
in the Text

Original editions of Amado's works are listed parenthetically after the edition I refer to in this study. Translations in the text are my own.

País — *O país do carnaval. Cacau. Suor.* 27th, 27th,
Cacau — and 26th eds., respectively. São Paulo: Martins,
Suor — 1971 (Rio de Janeiro: Schmidt, 1931; Rio de Janeiro: Ariel, 1933; and Rio de Janeiro: Ariel, 1934, respectively).

Jubiabá — *Jubiabá.* 26th ed. São Paulo: Martins, 1971 (Rio de Janeiro: José Olympio, 1935).

Mar — *Mar morto.* 28th ed. São Paulo: Martins, 1970 (Rio de Janeiro: José Olympio, 1936).

Capitães — *Capitães da areia.* 35th ed. São Paulo: Martins, 1973 (Rio de Janeiro: José Olympio, 1937).

Terras — *Terras do sem fim.* 7th ed. São Paulo: Martins, 1954 (São Paulo: Martins, 1943).

Ilhéus — *São Jorge dos Ilhéus.* 24th ed. São Paulo: Martins, 1971 (São Paulo: Martins, 1944).

Seara — *Seara vermelha.* 27th ed. São Paulo: Martins, 1972 (São Paulo: Martins, 1946).

Subterrâneos. — *Os subterrâneos da liberdade.* 25th ed. São Paulo: Martins, 1973 (São Paulo: Martins, 1954).

"Tempos" — 1. "Os ásperos tempos"

"Agonia" — 2. "Agonia da noite"

"Luz" — 3. "A luz no túnel"

Gabriela — *Gabriela, cravo e canela: Crônica de uma cidade do interior.* 29th ed. São Paulo: Martins, 1966 (São Paulo: Martins, 1958).

Os velhos marinheiros: Duas histórias do cais da Bahia. 17th ed. São Paulo: Martins, 1967 (São Paulo: Martins, 1961).

Quincas	1. *A morte e a morte de Quincas Berro D'água*
Comandante	2. *A completa verdade sobre as discutidas aventuras do comandante Vasco Moscoso de Aragão, capitão de longo curso* These two novelettes are currently published as separate volumes, the title of the second having been changed to *Os velhos marinheiros ou o capitão de longo curso.*
Pastores	*Os pastores da noite.* 17th ed. São Paulo: Martins, 1968 (São Paulo: Martins, 1964).
Dona Flor	*Dona Flor e seus dois maridos: História moral e de amor.* São Paulo: Martins, 1966 (first edition).
Tenda	*Tenda dos milagres.* São Paulo: Martins, 1969 (first edition).
Tereza	*Tereza Batista cansada de guerra.* São Paulo: Martins, 1972 (first edition).
Tieta	*Tieta do Agreste: Pastora de cabras ou a volta da filha pródiga, melodramático folhetim em cinco sensacionais episódios e comovente epílogo: Emoção e suspense!* Rio de Janeiro: Record, 1977 (first edition).
Farda	*Farda, fardão, camisola de dormir: Fábula para acender uma esperança.* 2nd. ed. Rio de Janeiro: Record, 1979 (Rio de Janeiro, Record, 1979).
Tocaia	*Tocaia Grande: A face obscura.* 7th ed. Rio de Janeiro: Record, 1986 (Rio de Janeiro, Record, 1984).
	O Sumiço da santa: Uma história de feitiçaria. Rio de Janeiro: Record, 1988 (first edition).

Chronology

1912   Jorge Amado born 10 August to Eulália Leal Amado de Faria and João Amado de Faria on the Auricídia cacao *fazenda* (farm), in the district of Ferradas, Itabuna county, southern Bahia, Brazil.

1913   Jorge unhurt, father wounded by would-be assassin's bullet in ambush at the Auricídia farm house.

1914   Flood destroys Auricídia. Family moves to Ferradas and then to Ilhéus, where father manages to open a sandal shop with little money saved.

1917   Family returns to cacao farming, setting up the Fazenda Tararanga. Father involved in Sequeiro Grande land disputes.

1918   Enrolls in school at Ilhéus, where family buys a second home. Attends trial arising out of Sequeiro Grande land disputes and is asked by judge to draw names of jurors. Brother Jofre born.

1920   Brother Joelson born.

1921   Death of brother Jofre.

1922   Enrolls in boarding school at Colégio Antônio Vieira in Salvador, Bahia. Brother James born.

1924   Runs away from boarding school to paternal grandfather's home in rural Sergipe state. Returns to family home in southern Bahia two months later.

1925   Enrolls in Colégio Ipiranga in Salvador.

1927   Works as reporter for *Diário da Bahia.*

1929   Publishes *Lenita,* a novel written with Dias da Costa and Édison Carneiro, in Rio de Janeiro.

1930   Moves to Rio de Janeiro to finish preparatory course. Getúlio Vargas takes power.

1931   Admitted to National Law School in Rio. Publishes first novel, *O país do carnaval.*

1933   Publishes *Cacau.* Marries Matilde Garcia Rosa.

1934   *Suor.*

1935   Daughter Lila born. Spanish translation of *Cacau* published in
        Buenos Aires. *Jubiabá* published. Finishes law school, but re-
        fuses to pick up diploma. Russian translations of *Cacau* and
        Suor.

1936   Jailed briefly in Rio by Vargas government over alleged support
        for abortive uprising in Natal in November, 1935. *Mar morto*
        garners Graça Aranha Prize.

1937   Travels to Rio Grande do Sul, Uruguay, Argentina, Chile,
        Mexico, and the U.S. Meets Diego Rivera, Orozco, Siqueiros,
        Michael Gold, and Paul Robeson. Publishes *Capitães da areia*
        in Rio. Jailed in Manaus. Public burning of his works in Sal-
        vador. Vargas imposes Estado Novo dictatorship.

1938   Taken to Rio and released. Travels to São Paulo and Sergipe.
        Book of poems, *A estrada do mar,* published.

1939   Returns to Rio.

1941   Goes into exile in Argentina. *ABC de Castro Alves* published in
        São Paulo by Martins.

1942   Publishes *Vida de Luiz Carlos Prestes, el caballero de la esperanza*
        in Buenos Aires. Collective novel, *Brandão entre o mar e o amor,*
        published in São Paulo. Jailed upon return to Brazil. Released
        upon condition he remain in Salvador.

1943   Campaigns in press for return to democracy. *Terras do sem fim*
        published.

1944   Legal separation from Matilde Garcia Rosa. Publishes *São Jorge
        dos Ilhéus.*

1945   Elected vice president of First Congress of Brazilian Writers.
        Brief imprisonment. Moves to São Paulo. Marries Zélia Gattai.
        Publishes *Bahia de Todos os Santos,* a guide to the city of Salva-
        dor. Vargas dictatorship falls. Amado elected to the Chamber
        of Deputies on the Communist party slate representing the
        state of São Paulo.

1946   Moves to Rio to assume duties as a federal deputy. Publishes
        Seara vermelha.

1947   Publication of play, *O amor de Castro Alves* (later called *O amor
        do soldado*). Son João Jorge born in Rio.

1948   Communist party outlawed; Amado removed from seat in
        Chamber of Deputies. Goes into self-exile in Europe. Takes up

residence in Paris. Contact with Sartre, Aragon, Éluard, Picasso, et al. Goes to Wrocław, Poland, as vice president of the World Congress of Writers and Artists for Peace. Meets Anna Seghers, Julien Huxley, Irene and Juliot Curie, Ilya Ehrenburg, and others. Travels to Italy, Czechoslovakia, Germany, Belgium, Switzerland, and the Soviet Union.

1949 Travels to Sweden, Norway, Denmark, Holland, Hungary, Bulgaria, etc. Airplane mishap in Germany. Daughter Lila dies suddenly in Rio.

1950 Sets up residence in a castle owned by the Czechoslovak Union of Writers in Dobris. Publishes in Brazil *O mundo da paz,* a book about travels to eastern-bloc countries, which is immediately branded as subversive.

1951 Daughter Paloma born in Prague. Receives Stalin Peace Prize in Moscow.

1952 Travels to China and Mongolia. Returns to Brazil. Charged as a result of his earlier publication of *O mundo da paz* with violation of national security laws; suit ends with no verdict. Travels in Brazil and Europe.

1953 Returns to Brazil. Death of a friend, the writer Graciliano Ramos. Trip to Europe.

1954 *Os subterrâneos da liberdade* (trilogy). Participates as special guest in Second Congress of Soviet Writers in Moscow.

1956 Assumes directorship of journal *Paratodos* in Rio.

1957 Travels in Far East.

1958 *Gabriela, cravo e canela* published, wins five major prizes.

1959 *A morte e a morte de Quincas Berro D'água* published in the magazine *Senhor.* Investment as dignitary in Axé Opô Afonjá, an important *candomblé* congregation in Salvador.

1961 Elected to the Brazilian Academy of Letters. Publishes *Os velhos marinheiros.*

1962 Death of father. Visits Cuba and Mexico.

1963 Takes up residence in Salvador, Bahia.

1964 Military takeover of the Brazilian government. *Os pastores da noite.*

1966 *Dona Flor e seus dois maridos.*

1969   *Tenda dos milagres.*

1971   Travels to U.S. and Canada. Writer in residence at Pennsylvania State University. Return to Brazil.

1972   Death of mother. *Tereza Batista cansada de guerra.*

1976   Residence in London. Return to Brazil. Film version of *Dona Flor e seus dois maridos.* Publication of *O gato malhado e a andorinha sinhá* (written in 1948 for his son João Jorge).

1977   Publication of *Tieta do Agreste.* Film version of *Tenda dos milagres.*

1979   *Farda, fardão, camisola de dormir.*

1981   *O menino grapiúna* (memoirs of early years).

1984   *Tocaia Grande.*

1985   Return of civilian government in Brazil.

1987   Jorge Amado Cultural Foundation opens in Salvador, Bahia.

1988   *O sumiço da santa.*

Chapter One
Writer, Social Critic, and Politician

> From my mother's telling it so many times, the scene became as vivid and real to me as if I had actually retained some memory of it. . . . Ten months old, I was crawling on the farmhouse veranda toward the end of sunset. . . . My father was cutting some cane for the mare, his favorite mount. The gunman, hiding behind a guava tree, rested his repeater in the fork of its branches . . . awaiting the right moment to fire it. . . . The animal caught the fatal bullet, [but] pieces of lead embedded in [Father's] shoulders and back. . . . [He] was just able to pick up his son and carry him into the kitchen, where Dona Eulália was fixing dinner. He handed her the boy all covered with his father's blood.

So begins Amado's account of his childhood in southern Bahia amid the land wars and boomtown violence of the turn-of-the-century Brazilian frontier (*O menino grapiúna* [Boy from southern Bahia], 11–14). Like his father, João Amado de Faria, who, Amado states, was to carry the debris of this shooting in his body for the rest of his days, the future writer, social critic, and politician would not forget the baptism of blood of his mother's story. He would preserve many of his memories and the tales of others' memories of these early years in his later fiction, along with the experiences of his youth among the poor and marginalized of Salvador and the Bahian interior. Indeed, such violence, whether spawned by the cacao wars, wrought by severities of climate and disease, or perpetrated upon the poor by a landed elite, was to make an indelible imprint on his works from the very beginning. And it was to remain a watchword of his fiction until the present day.

Born on 10 August 1912 to Eulália Leal Amado de Faria and João Amado de Faria on their cacao *fazenda* (farm, plantation) in rural southern Bahia, Jorge was to experience several other harrowing incidents and tragedies before his tenth birthday. In 1914 the Cachoeira River overflowed its banks and destroyed vast tracts of cacao plants, among

them the Amados' Fazenda Auricídia. The family first took refuge in
an abandoned infirmary in nearby Ferradas that had once housed lepers
and smallpox patients. From there, the Amados moved into Ilhéus, to
a poor section of town, where João and Eulália were able eventually to
earn a living by making and selling sandals and to scrape together the
wherewithal to purchase a new plot and resume cacao planting. It was
here that João would become involved in the land disputes of the Sequeiro Grande region. From his bedroom window the boy would watch
the bands of gunmen come and go with his father in the lead, the fear
of bloodshed ever present.

A smallpox epidemic struck the area in 1918. Few escaped entirely,
and those who managed to recover from the dreaded disease were used
to carry the newly infected in burlap bags to the lazaretto. Amado was
left with lasting memories of such scenes, which he would later weave
into the plots of such novels as *Capitães da areia* (1937), *Seara vermelha*
(1946), and *Tereza Batista cansada de guerra* (1972). That same year
young Jorge, in the company of his father, attended a trial that had
arisen out of the Sequeiro Grande land disputes and was asked by the
presiding judge to draw the names of the jurors, an episode he would
later describe in *Terras do sem fim* (1943; *The Violent Land,* 1945). Also
in 1918 brother Jofre was born, only to die three years later after the
birth of a third son, Joelson.

At the age of six Amado was enrolled in the grammar school of Dona
Guilhermina in Ilhéus, where the family, now more prosperous, had
purchased a second home. Dona Guilhermina would later appear as a
schoolmarm celebrated for her severity in both *Terras do sem fim* and
Gabriela, cravo e canela (1958; *Gabriela, Clove and Cinnamon,* 1962).
Following the death of Jofre, Jorge was sent to Salvador as a boarding
student at Colégio Antônio Vieira. He was ten years old. Shortly thereafter, his brother James was born. While at Antônio Vieira, Jorge was
taken under the wing of Father Luís Gonzaga Cabral, a Portuguese
Jesuit priest and teacher who was famed as a homilist. It was Father
Cabral who introduced him to the Portuguese romantics Garrett and
Herculano and to British authors such as Swift, Scott, and Dickens. A
brief flirtation with mysticism was followed by a period of depression,
in which Jorge expressed a desire to leave the *colégio.* In 1924, unable
to persuade his father to transfer him from Antônio Vieira to another
school, he set off alone and virtually penniless through the backlands
of Bahia, eventually making his way to the home of his grandfather,
José Amado, in the state of Sergipe, where he stayed for two months

before having to return to the family *fazenda*. This escapade proved to be one of the highlights of his young life, for it put him in closer touch with the working classes, who would later become the primary focus of many of his novels.

The following year he entered the Colégio Ipiranga in Salvador, whose director, Isaías Alves de Almeida, afforded his boarding students a greater degree of freedom than was to be had at Antônio Vieira. Here the young teenager devoured the works of Balzac and Maupassant, of the South Americans Ingenieros, Rodó, and Vargas Vila, and of Brazilian modernists such as Menotti del Picchia and Oswald de Andrade. Here, too, he made his first attempts at writing prose fiction. Modernism had come to Brazil in 1922 with the celebration of the Modern Art Week in February of that year, and had quickly spread from its focal point in São Paulo to Rio and to the country's provincial capitals.

At the age of fifteen, Amado ceased boarding at the *colégio* and went to work as a reporter for the *Diário da Bahia*. He began to write poetry, short stories, and essays for literary magazines and joined a circle of young writers who had congregated around the symbolist poet Pinheiro Viegas. His experiences in this group would later form the basis for his first work of fiction, a novelette, entitled *O país do carnaval* (The land of carnival), published by poet Augusto Frederico Schmidt in Rio in 1931. In 1928 he took up residence in the Pelourinho district of downtown Salvador, where he began writing a short novel about the exploitation of the city's tenement dwellers. But *Suor* (Sweat) would not be completed and published until 1934. In the meantime, he penned another short novel, *Lenita* (1929), in collaboration with two friends, Dias da Costa and Édison Carneiro, and moved to Rio, where he published *O país do carnaval* after finishing a preparatory course and entering the National Law School. Here he quickly became involved in the Carioca literary circles and, after a brief trip to the Northeast, where he met novelists Graciliano Ramos and José Lins do Rego and renewed his acquaintance with Rachel de Queiroz, he returned to Rio and redoubled his writing and publishing efforts. He also tried his hand at another short novel, the contemporary, rural proletarian *Cacau* (Cacao), which was brought out in 1933, shortly before his marriage to Matilde Garcia Rosa.

It was to Matilde that Amado dedicated his first full-dress novel, *Jubiabá,* in 1935. Earlier that year a daughter, Lila, had been born to the couple, and a Spanish translation of *Cacau,* the first of many translations of the author's books, had been published in Buenos Aires. The novel revolved around the upbringing of Antônio Balduíno, a black youth, on the streets of Salvador and his adventures and self-education as a young man. It minced no words in its stark portrayal of vice and poverty and was immediately hailed as a masterpiece by Brazilian critics, becoming one of the two best-sellers of the year, alongside Lins do Rego's *O moleque Ricardo* (Black boy Richard). Although the three earlier works had received favorable comments, *Jubiabá* was especially applauded for its inclusion of Afro-Brazilian religious elements in its portrayal of the Bahian *candomblé* (Afro-Bahian religious cult) of Pai Jubiabá, a former slave. Like *Cacau*, it was a rural proletarian novel, set partly in the interior of the state, where the protagonist had gone to work on a tobacco farm. Like *Suor*, it dealt with the oppression of the urban proletariat in Salvador, culminating in a dockworkers' strike led by the novel's hero, who becomes a political activist. To these elements was added another, the valorization of African culture. Thus, *Jubiabá* was regarded as a significant step in the development of the modern novel of the Brazilian Northeast, which had begun to flourish with the publication of José Américo de Almeida's *A bagaceira* (Cane trash) in 1928 and Rachel de Queiroz's *O quinze* (The year fifteen) in 1930.

Later that year Amado finished law school but declined to pick up his diploma. Russian translations of *Cacau* and *Suor* were brought out in Moscow. In 1936 and again in 1937 the author published urban social novels set in Salvador. The first of these, *Mar morto* (*Sea of Death*, 1984), was concerned with the hardships of the city's small transport-boat owners. Like *Jubiabá*, it focused on the poor and featured Afro-Brazilian customs and beliefs. Several strong female characters are prominent in the novel, which also stressed the seamy side of the characters' lives and the violence to which they were daily subjected. But, unlike the earlier works, it did so with a heavy dose of lyricism, which led some to see it as romanticizing poverty and consequently diminishing the very characters to whom it purported to pay tribute. Others saw this lyric quality, though, as an asset, and many came to regard the novel as one of Amado's best.

The second novel, *Capitães da areia* (*Captains of the Sands*, 1988) shared many of these qualities with its immediate predecessor. It too dealt with the lives of the underdogs and placed emphasis upon popular and Afro-Bahian culture. Following the example of the first part of *Jubiabá*, it depicted the lives of a gang of street waifs in the Salvador of the 1930s. Yet it was more militant in its attack on Brazilian social problems, placing the blame for much of the city's juvenile delinquency at the doorstep of the authorities and of an inadequate correctional system, famous for its brutality. The prose narration was interspersed with fictional newspaper headlines, letters to the editor, and journalistic accounts, thus enriching the novelistic discourse with a series of alternative voices.

After a brief imprisonment in Rio in 1936 on the pretext that he had somehow supported an abortive military revolt against the Vargas regime the year before, Amado had traveled to southern Brazil in 1937 to see Érico Veríssimo and then to Uruguay, Argentina, Chile, Peru, Ecuador, Colombia, Guatemala, Cuba, Mexico, and the United States. During his trip he made the acquaintance of a number of Spanish-American writers and of the Mexican muralists Diego Rivera, David Alfaro Siqueiros, and José Clemente Orozco. In the United States he met with novelist Michael Gold, whose *Jews without Money* (1930) had been a major influence on his own *Suor,* with Waldo Frank, the American intellectual, and with entertainer and social activist Paul Robeson. Upon his return in October 1937 he was arrested in Manaus and his books were banned nationwide. Thousands of copies were publicly burned in Salvador and São Paulo, along with the works of other authors, in early November. Within a week, Getúlio Vargas proclaimed the Estado Novo (New State) dictatorship.

In January 1938 Amado was taken to Rio and released. He went to São Paulo and spent several months there unemployed before traveling to Estância, Sergipe, where he spent the rest of the year. There he published a book of poems, *A estrada do mar.* In 1939, with the outbreak of World War II, Amado returned to Rio, where he resumed his literary activities. But because of the atmosphere of oppression that prevailed in the Brazil of the Estado Novo, he decided to move to Argentina two years later. While he was living in Buenos Aires, his *ABC de Castro Alves* (ABC of Castro Alves), a biography of the Bahian romantic poet, was published in São Paulo by Livraria Martins Editora (1941), which would continue to be his Brazilian publisher for the next thirty-four years.

The following year, *Vida de Luiz Carlos Prestes, el caballero de la esperanza* (The life of Luiz Carlos Prestes, the knight of hope), his biography of the imprisoned Brazilian communist leader, was published in Buenos Aires, and a collective novel, *Brandão entre o mar e o amor* (Brandão, between the sea and love), written in collaboration with Graciliano Ramos, José Lins do Rego, Rachel de Queiroz, and Aníbal

Machado, was published in São Paulo. In August 1942 Brazil declared war against the Axis powers, and the following month Amado attempted to return to Brazil. Arrested shortly after his arrival in Porto Alegre, he was again imprisoned in Rio and released in November on the condition that he remain in Salvador. With the new year he began work as a journalist for *O imparcial,* a Bahian newspaper, where he would spend the next two years writing a daily column about the war. During this period he also campaigned in the press for a return to democratic government.

Terras do sem fim (The Violent Land) was published in 1943. Written the year before, while the author was living in Montevideo, Uruguay, it was extraordinarily well received and to this day is considered by many critics to be Amado's masterpiece. Like *Cacau,* it was set in the cacao-growing region of southern Bahia, but in the earlier period of 1911–12, when the feuding over the Sequeiro Grande had just begun and cacao barons fought with one another to carve up the new lands and establish political and economic dynasties. Indeed, it delved much more deeply than *Cacau* into the social fabric of the region, portraying both rich and poor with a greater degree of objectivity than the novelist had achieved previously. Gone were the black-and-white, often cardboard characterizations of many of the immature works. The myriad of human types—the planters, gamblers, adventurers, hired gunmen, laborers, and prostitutes drawn to the region by King Cacao—were all treated with a mixture of critical detachment, mild reproof, and sympathy. As he had done in *Mar morto,* Amado included several strong female characters among the dramatis personae. Likewise, he tempered frank, sometimes crude descriptions of the frontier lifestyle with liberal doses of lyricism and humor. Moreover, he relied more heavily on his childhood experiences and on the accounts of relatives and the backwoods storytellers with whom he had grown up to chronicle the hardships and horrors of the times.

In December 1944 Amado was legally separated from Matilde Garcia Rosa and saw the publication of *São Jorge dos Ilhéus,* intended as a sequel to his best-seller of the previous year. However, the novel did not fare as well as its predecessor with the Brazilian critics and reading public. In January 1945 Amado was elected vice president of the First Congress of Brazilian Writers, convening in São Paulo. When the meeting turned into a demonstration against the dictatorship, the novelist was thrown into jail. Later freed, he took up residence in São Paulo, where he married Zélia Gattai on 8 July. There, on the occasion of Prestes's release from prison, he met Pablo Neruda, with whom he struck up a friendship that was to last until the Chilean poet's death in 1973. Both were on the podium with the Brazilian communist leader at the political rally called to commemorate the latter's freedom. In September, the novelist's *Bahia de Todos os Santos* (Bahia of All Saints), a guide to the city of Salvador, was published by Martins, along with several of his earlier works. With the fall of the Vargas regime at the end of November, political parties were again legalized and Amado was elected to the Chamber of Deputies on the Communist party ticket as a representative of São Paulo state.

In 1946 he moved to Rio to assume his duties as a federal deputy in what was then the national capital. He finished and published another novel, *Seara vermelha* (Red harvest), which recounted the sufferings of a migrant family fleeing the country's drought-ridden interior. Unabashedly political in its sympathies and often regarded as less accomplished than Graciliano Ramos's earlier novelistic treatment of the same topic in *Vidas secas* (1938; *Barren Lives*), *Seara vermelha* was, nonetheless, a success with the reading public, becoming one of the most translated of the writer's works, particularly in the Eastern-bloc countries. In September, as a delegate to the constitutional convention, Amado was one of the signers of the 1946 Brazilian constitution. And in 1947 he published a play entitled *O amor de Castro Alves* (The love of Castro Alves, later renamed *O amor do soldado* [The love of the soldier]), for which he was awarded a medal commemorating the centenary of the poet Alves's birth. In November his son João Jorge was born in Rio de Janeiro.

These were tumultuous years for Amado. His congressional responsibilities and political activism often left little time for writing. He introduced several congressional bills beneficial to culture and promoting the collective interests of Brazilian writers. He was also a popular speaker at political rallies and on several occasions undertook speaking tours to various states to bolster the strength of the party. One such trip was a veritable nightmare, writes Zélia Gattai in her autobiography of her early years with the novelist, *Um chapéu para viagem* (A hat for traveling).[1] After a string of successful rallies in Salvador, Recife, and Fortaleza, the Amados traveled to a small town in the interior of Ceará, where Jorge had been invited to address a party meeting. It turned out that there were no more than a handful of supporters in the town. The rest of the inhabitants were openly hostile to the cause. Some swore death to the communists and to Amado, pledging to defend Christianity against the agents of Satan. A mob formed and, at the instigation of a parish priest, who plied the crowd with liquor, the Amados were assaulted and had to take refuge in a boarding house; they were finally able to escape several hours later in a truck owned by a local sympathizer.

The Communist party had been outlawed in May 1947, and in early 1948 Amado was removed from his seat in the Chamber of Deputies. He went into voluntary exile in Europe, establishing residence in the Latin Quarter of Paris. Here, he came into contact with a large number of European writers and artists, among them Jean-Paul Sartre, Louis Aragon, Paul Éluard, and Pablo Picasso, and became a close friend of American émigré Michael Gold, whom he had earlier met during his trip to the United States. "Jorge and Mike were inseparable," writes Zélia Gattai in *Um chapéu para viagem.*[2] "Together, they took part in congresses and writers' conferences in several parts of the world." In August Amado traveled to Wrocław, Poland, as vice president of the World Congress of Writers and Artists for Peace. Among the participants he met were Anna Seghers, Julien Huxley, Irene and Juliot Curie, Salvatore Quasimodo, and Ilya Ehrenburg. In December he journeyed to Italy, Czechoslovakia, Germany, Belgium, Switzerland, and the Soviet Union. And in January 1949 he traveled to Sweden, Norway, Denmark, Holland, Hungary, Bulgaria, and several other countries that he had previously visited. In March he was involved in an airplane mishap in Germany; in December his daughter Lila died suddenly in Rio at the age of fifteen.

A month later Amado moved his family to Czechoslovakia, where he established residence in Dobris in a castle owned by the Czechoslovakian Union of Writers. Here, the following August (1951), his daughter Paloma was born. In December he went to Moscow to receive the Stalin Peace Prize, and in January 1952 he traveled to China and Mongolia, returning to Brazil several months later. He had published in Brazil in 1950 *O mundo da paz* (The world of peace), a book about his travels in the Eastern-bloc countries. It had immediately been branded as subversive by the Brazilian authorities and Amado had been prosecuted for allegedly violating the national security law. Upon his return home in 1952 the suit was revived, only to end inconclusively a short time later. After traveling to several parts of Brazil, Amado returned to Europe in December.

In March 1953 he went back to Brazil and shortly thereafter made a trip to Argentina and Chile. Upon receiving word that his friend the novelist Graciliano Ramos was in grave condition, he rushed back to Rio, where Ramos died a few days later. Amado again traveled to Europe in October, but returned to Brazil a month later. The following May saw the publication of *Os subterrâneos da liberdade* (The freedom underground), his trilogy about the role of the Brazilian Communist party during the Estado Novo. Many of the characters and scenes of this work were based on reality, and the protagonist, Mariana Azevedo, and her family bore a striking resemblance to Zélia and the Gattais. Later in 1954 the novelist attended the Second Congress of Soviet Writers in Moscow as an invited guest.

In 1956 Amado became the director of the cultural journal *Paratodos* in Rio. After a trip to Asia and Europe in 1957 he returned to Brazil, where he stunned the literary world in 1958 with the publication of *Gabriela, cravo e canela* (*Gabriela, Clove and Cinnamon*), which won five major prizes and sold 100,000 copies in a little over a year. Appearing just four years after *Subterrâneos,* widely recognized as his most political work, *Gabriela* had nothing of the partisan polemics to which Amado's readers had become accustomed. Like *São Jorge dos Ilhéus,* it dealt with life in the cacao-growing region of southern Bahia in the period just following the events recounted in *Terras do sem fim.* Yet, it did so in a lighthearted, satirical manner, which some critics labeled "picaresque," employing irony, tongue-in-cheek humor, and camp, archaizing chapter and section titles. Characters were not extolled or condemned, as in previous works, but treated with a sympathetic smile despite their shortcomings as human beings. Rather than proclaiming the need for political revolution, the novel chronicled the region's transition from a late feudal to an early capitalist economy by tracing the evolution of its political practices and sexual mores. Female characters were seen as primary indicators of the social changes at work in the novel. And its protagonist, Gabriela, a woman of humble origins, was seen more as a salutary but unwitting catalyst of such changes than as a politically aware heroine of the working classes.

The year 1959 marked Amado's investment as a lay dignitary in Axé Opô Afonjá, an important *candomblé* congregation in the Bahian capital. Years later, responding to a reader's question about whether he believed in the Afro-Brazilian religion, he would write:

I am a materialist, but my materialism does not reduce me, does not castrate me, does not diminish me with the pettiness of dogmas that limit human experience as much as any religion or sect. . . . Thus, I can sit happily in my chair as a dignitary in the Axé Opô Afonjá, covered with necklaces, clothed with authority and honor, which were bestowed on me by my friends in the Afro-Bahian religions. . . . Only thus, through real and profound experience, not through the simple observation of a reporter, will I be qualified to speak to you of the *orixás* [African divinities] and the lives of common people, of the mysteries and magic of Bahia. Only thus will I be able to re-create their truth, to re-create the faces of the men and women who surround me, whose feet fashion the most beautiful dance, men and women who brought from the depths of slavery, on their injured shoulders, such beauty that they have rescued and preserved for us.[3]

In 1961 Amado was accorded another honor: he was elected unanimously to the Brazilian Academy of Letters, to the seat once occupied by the first president, Machado de Assis. As he was initiated, on the thirtieth anniversary of the publication of *O país do carnaval,* he declared:

I have always sought the uncomfortable road of commitment to the poor and the oppressed, to those who have nothing, who struggle for a place in the sun, to those who do not partake of worldly goods, and I have tried to be, insofar as I could, a voice for their longings, sorrows, and hopes. . . . Many times, I have been accused of being biased and partial, of being a committed writer, one who is limited by such commitments, of being a political, participating writer. This charge has never hurt me or brought me sorrow; I have never been offended by it. What writer is not political? I know of none.[4] ("Discurso de Posse na Academia Brasileira," *Jorge Amado, povo e terra: 40 anos de literatura,* 13)

In 1959 the novelist had published in the magazine *Senhor* a novelette entitled *A morte e a morte de Quincas Berro D'água* (*The Two Deaths of Quincas Wateryell,* 1965), which recounted the picaresque adventures of a middle-class man who had abandoned a boring existence as a respectable husband and father to run with whores and sharpers. Two years later, the work was included, along with another novelette, *A completa verdade sobre as discutidas aventuras do comandante Vasco Moscoso de Aragão, capitão de longo curso* (*Home Is the Sailor,* 1964), in a single volume with the title *Os velhos marinheiros* (The old sailors). (Later, the works would be published in separate volumes, with the latter assuming the title *Os velhos marinheiros ou o capitão de longo curso.*) The two works continued in the satirical tone set by *Gabriela,* now turning to an exploration of the relativity of truth, in a juxtaposition of the multiple realities associated with their respective protagonists. Like *Quincas,* the second novelette told the story of a man with a dual identity. But, whereas the mystery of Quincas Berro D'água resided not in the truth or falsehood of the hero's two personas but in the bizarre circumstances surrounding his death, the enigma of Vasco Moscoso lay precisely in that identity. He was either a retired seafaring hero or a shameless impostor. The acceptance of one version of the truth seemed to preclude the other. And, although Amado sometimes appeared to favor one of the two, he was always careful to offset this with an apparent preference for its opposite. Such was the skillfulness of the two tales, which lacked much of the digressive wordiness associated with many of the novelist's latter-day works, that for many years *Quincas* and *Comandante* have enjoyed the highest reputation among many Amadian literary critics.

In 1962 the writer traveled to Cuba and Mexico shortly after the death of his father, João Amado de Faria. And in 1963 he and his family returned to Salvador to take up permanent residence there. *Os pastores da noite (Shepherds of the Night,* 1967) was published in July of the following year, just three months after the military takeover of the government. It, like *Quincas,* focused on the lives of the ne'er-do-wells populating Salvador's *bas-fonds.* In fact, it continued the stories of several of Quincas's skid-row companions, from Cabo Martim's ill-fated marriage to an ingenious solution to a baptismal problem provided by Exu, the Yoruban trickster divinity, and finally to a violent confrontation between police and squatters, in which the latter prevail by outwitting their opponents. Critical reaction to *Pastores* was not as enthusiastic as it had been to the previous two works. Some critics objected to what they regarded as the esoteric nature of the author's use of *candomblé* ritual in the baptismal episode, while others felt the triptych lacked the vitality of its predecessors. And, more than ever before, there were those who saw the work as a simplistic romanticizing of backwardness, a trivialization of poverty that exploited the working classes. Amado was even the target of a defamation-of-character suit brought by a local fortuneteller, who saw herself depicted in one of the novel's characters.

Dona Flor e seus dois maridos (Dona Flor and Her Two Husbands) came out in 1966. It was the story of a lower middle-class cooking teacher in the Salvador of the 1920s and 1930s whose second marriage to a respectable but insipid pharmacist was haunted by the ghost of her roguish, profligate first husband. The desultory text, which ran close to five hundred pages, was larded with skillfully blended recipes and menus featuring many of the spicy dishes for which Afro-Bahian cuisine is noted. Like *Quincas,* the work satirized the excesses and hypocrisies of the Brazilian bourgeoisie. Moreover, almost half of the more than three hundred characters in the novel were taken from real life, many retaining their actual names. Thus, *Dona Flor* could be said to constitute a roman à clef of sorts, but one in which most of the real-life characters were treated in a jocular fashion rather than being ridiculed or reproached. Yet below this veneer of frivolity there was much more to the novel. The two husbands, so diametrically opposed to each other, might be regarded as metaphors for two contradictory *ethoi* or political forces. The heroine's magical solution, affording her the best of both Vadinho and Teodoro, as well as the drama leading up to it, could also be taken on a sociopolitical level, particularly in light of the grave political developments of the preceding few years. The work could thus be read as a statement about the problems of and direction to be followed by the Brazilian people.

Bahia boa terra Bahia (Bahia the good land Bahia), a photo album of Salvador prepared by the author in collaboration with artist Carybé and photographer Flávio Damm, appeared in 1967. In 1969 Amado published *Tenda dos milagres* (*Tent of Miracles,* 1971), which, albeit largely satirical in tone, was at times a bitter denunciation of the violence and racism to which Brazilian blacks have traditionally been subjected. Episodes from the life of Pedro Archanjo, a turn-of-the-century black autodidact and university beadle plagued by racial discrimination, were alternated with scenes of the 1969 preparations for the centennial of his birth. The juxtaposition and resulting ironic contrapuntal structure served to lay bare the continuing bigotry and hypocrisy of white, upper-class Brazilians, more concerned with fashion and profits than with righting injustice or achieving historical accuracy. And although the novelist's use of a bumbling, dramatized narrator, similar to the one he had employed in *Comandante,* lent a measure of humor to the narrative, *Tenda* was, in the end, a much more somber book than any of the other works the novelist had written since 1958. Likewise, it was given to sermonizing, and some critics saw in it a tendency to revert to the largely Manichean characterizations of earlier Amadian fiction.

In 1971, after returning from a trip to Europe, the Amados traveled extensively in the United States and Canada, where the novelist spent the months of October and November as writer-in-residence at Pennsylvania State University. In December the Amados' first grandchild was born in Salvador. The following year marked the death of Eulália Leal Amado de Faria, the author's mother, as well as the birth of the Amados' second grandchild in Rio de Janeiro. It was also the year of *Tereza Batista cansada de guerra (Tereza Batista: Home from the Wars*, 1975), which recounted the ordeals of a Bahian prostitute in a parodic stylization of the Brazilian folk poetry known as *literatura de cordel* ("string literature," after the vendors' habit of hanging the pulp leaflets from a length of twine). Complete with such *cordel*-like trappings as long, enumerative section titles, introductory woodcuts, and abecedarian poetic form, the work employed a heavy dose of fantasy, hyperbole, and humor, a number of formulaic plot motifs, and multiple narrators, among them the author's late mother. There was, as usual, a wealth of sexual episodes, culminating in a prostitutes' strike suffused with a circuslike atmosphere. Many of the characters were wooden caricatures, and they were often juxtaposed with real-life and historical personages, as was the novelist's custom.

More than his previous novels, *Tereza* was the target of denunciation by several of the younger literary critics. Despite the usual accolades with which many admiring reviewers greeted the work, there were those who saw in it the novelist's misogyny and sadistic fascination with the sexual exploitation of the protagonist. Others accused him of legitimizing the backwardness and ignorance of poor Brazilians—a charge heard before—while still others alleged that he continued to overvalue raw instinct and human sexuality to the detriment of the human mind. One critic denounced the characterization of Tereza Batista on the grounds that it was an androcentric idealization of the prostitute with no basis in reality. Another felt that the novelist's use of farcical humor to describe the strike episode had the effect of trivializing the prostitutes' struggle against exploitation.[5] Many, however, objected not so much to the subject matter of *Tereza* and others of Amado's works as to their structure, which they regarded as founded on timeworn nineteenth-century models.

After a short residence in London in 1976 to complete the manuscript of *Tieta do Agreste (Tieta the Goat Girl*, 1979), his next novel, Amado returned to Brazil, where he published *O gato malhado e a andorinha sinhá (The Swallow and the Tom Cat*, 1982), a children's tale written in 1948 for his one-year-old son. November 1976 marked the premiere of *Dona Flor e seus dois maridos*, a motion picture starring Sônia Braga. With *Tieta* still unfinished, he returned to London, where in

April of 1977 he completed the novel before going back to Brazil. Published in August with great fanfare by Editora Record of Rio de Janeiro, the work was followed two months later by the premiere of the film version of *Tenda dos milagres*. A film of *Os pastores da noite* also made its debut in 1977.

Like *Tereza, Tieta* dealt with the life of a prostitute, but one who had achieved success as a madam in São Paulo and now sought to return to her hometown in northeastern Brazil. Despite its apparent frivolity—the plot and much of the humor derive from the clash of puritan and liberated ways—the novel attempted to address in the usual Amadian carnivalized fashion such serious questions as environmental pollution, internal colonialism, and priestly celibacy. Critical reaction, however, was much the same as it had been for the previous book—lavish praise on the part of longtime admirers, but a growing chorus of dissatisfaction from a number of younger critics, who charged that the novelist was pandering to the unsophisticated tastes of the literary marketplace.

In 1979 Amado published *Farda, fardão, camisola de dormir* (*Pen, Sword, Camisole,* 1985), which told the story of a clever campaign to deny a seat in the Brazilian Academy of Letters to a military man at the height of the Vargas dictatorship. Set in Rio de Janeiro—the first of the author's novels to unfold entirely outside Bahia since *Os subterrâneos da liberdade* in 1954—the work was received less than enthusiastically by many literary critics, both young and old. Later in 1979 Amado traveled to Senegal at the invitation of President Léopold Senghor and visited Angola as a guest of the country's first president, Agostinho Neto. In 1981 he celebrated his fiftieth anniversary as a novelist, publishing the memoirs of his childhood in southern Bahia, *O menino grapiúna*.

Tocaia Grande (*Showdown,* 1988) came out in 1984. In it Amado returned to the land of cacao, to the frontier violence of his early years, which had previously given us *Terras do sem fim*. The book narrates the story of the settlement of an interior Bahian town around the turn of the century and is replete with the land wars, epidemics, and colorful backwoods characters of the earlier work. Like his later fiction, it is also characterized by ribaldry, picaresque humor, and magic realism. Yet the novelist again seeks to deal with a serious issue: the underside of history as opposed to the official version. He shows how, time and again, the poor and ignorant have been dispossessed not only of their lands but of their rightful place in history as the tamers of the frontier, the real protagonists—how the "obscure face" of history has been re-pressed by the canonical discourse.

Civilian government returned to Brazil in 1985. Amado was one of the most vocal opponents of censorship during the military regime, refusing to submit his works to censors for their approval. In 1987 the Jorge Amado Cultural Foundation opened in the Pelourinho district of downtown Salvador, Bahia. The author's latest novel, *O sumiço da santa*, was published in 1988.

Chapter Two
The Early Amado: A Honing of Tools

Amadian Social Realism: An Overview

Gilberto Freyre, the late Brazilian social historian and novelist, once described Jorge Amado, along with José Lins do Rego, as "master caricaturists, not photographic realists." Likening them both in this respect to such earlier Brazilian artists and writers as Aleijadinho, Gregório de Matos, and Euclides da Cunha, he observed that "though keenly alive to reality, each of these two most famous novelists of modern Brazil is a mixture of the artist and the social critic; each is a poet in prose; each, though possibly deficient in sophisticated humor, is a powerful master of caricature and satire of the kind that simple men can understand."[1]

In his early works Amado grappled constantly with the problem of striking a balance between "social document" and "literature." His initial attempts, which he seemed to regard as "proletarian novels," were weighted heavily in favor of exposing societal inequities, often to the detriment of artistic quality. Others of the author's juvenilia were seen as attenuating social criticism with their predominant lyrical cast and their idealization of exotic Afro-Brazilian and folk culture. Yet from an early date Amado's fiction was indeed characterized by the sorts of syntheses that Freyre noted. Even in the novels of the 1940s and early 1950s, where political considerations seemed to predominate, the author's tendencies toward crude realism and denunciation of social ills were mitigated by the presence of lyricism, humor, and caricature.

To be sure, Amadian "social realism" was motivated first and foremost by a desire to correct social injustice. The novelist's early fiction combined hard-hitting exposé with frank, often explicit description of the seamy side of the lives of the Bahian underclasses. Patterning his works on the neonaturalistic and proletarian fiction of the 1930s in Europe and the United States, Amado was highly praised as a spokesman for the poor, the downtrodden, the underdog of society, much as novelists like Steinbeck, Erskine Caldwell, and Michael Gold were in this country. Books such as *Cacau, Jubiabá, Terras do sem fim, São Jorge dos Ilhéus,* and *Seara vermelha* focused on the lives of rural peasants and the abuses brought about by the traditional land-tenure system of the Brazilian interior. Many of them also dealt with such matters as land struggles, boomtown violence, drought, epidemics, banditry, migration, and messianic religious movements. Other works, such as *Suor, Jubiabá, Mar morto, Capitães da areia,* and the trilogy *Os subterrâneos da liberdade,* decried the hardships of the urban proletariat and lumpenproletariat of the Bahian capital or other cities. Among the topics they treated were slum conditions, corruption, racism, juvenile delinquency, and the exploitation of workers. Many culminated in victorious strike scenes or similar demonstrations of popular strength. Whether primarily rural or urban in their setting, however, such works tended to view society in terms of social classes. Characters were represented not so much as individuals but as typical representatives of the classes to which they belonged. What is more, working-class characters were usually depicted as virtuous, while exponents of the ruling elite were limned as unsavory and cruel.

One prevalent element that was often associated with the novelist's social realism was his liberal use of profanity and frequent inclusion of sexual and scatological scenes. In a 1951 essay Miécio Táti saw in some of Amado's early works an excessive emphasis on the salacious, which he felt negated their proletarian claims.[2] Apparently anticipating that a portion of his readership would be offended by such textual practices, the novelist himself had declared that he was not a pornographer or a muckraker in the "Explanation" to his first book, *O país do carnaval.* That some literary critics were unimpressed by the disclaimer is not surprising, however, for in recent memory only a few Brazilian novelists, such as the naturalists Aluísio Azevedo and Adolfo Caminha, had injected such a concentration of bawdy details into their literature, but without the earthy vocabulary that had become Amado's hallmark. Even the ribaldry so prevalent in Mário de Andrade's *Macunaíma* and Oswald de Andrade's *Serafim Ponte Grande* had been tempered by its appearance in a humorous, satirical context. No doubt, a great deal of Amado's initial coarseness could be laid to his desire to exploit its inherent shock value. He was attempting to elicit the reader's sympathy for the underprivileged classes by portraying their socioeconomic oppression in all of its neonaturalistic sordidness. One could argue, too, that profanity was an integral part of the vocabulary of those segments of society he was wont to portray and as such constituted an essential facet of his social realism. Yet there was still the perception, not only on the part of the more prudish Brazilian critics but also on that of many of Amado's admirers and ideological fellows, that his use of such practices was excessive.

To the extent that it tended to obscure his political message, another element, the novelist's penchant for lyricism, also sometimes drew fire from his Marxist allies. This was particularly the case with *Mar morto* and to some degree with *Jubiabá*. Yet more often it was cited by critics of various persuasions as one of the author's major literary assets, one of the most effective vehicles by which he pressed his arguments. Far from blunting his social criticism, Amado's flair for waxing poetic served to reinforce the narrow documentary aspect of his fiction, rendering it more palatable and persuasive. Along with such devices as characterization and plot development, lyric description of the sea, the tropical forest, and the rituals of *candomblé* was one of the chief factors differentiating the author's works from journalistic reportage or social and political tracts. From it derived much of the forcefulness and appeal of his novels.

Like ribaldry, humor *lato sensu* and caricature played a signal role in Amado's social realism from the very beginning. Aside from the often witty persiflage of the young intellectuals depicted in *O país do carnaval*, most of the incidences of humor in the early works were indeed associated with coarseness or caricature, as Freyre indicates. Off-color stories frequently possessed class overtones in these books; they targeted the ruling elites and often functioned as social wish fulfillments of sorts. Such was the case not only in works like *Cacau* and *Jubiabá* but also in *São Jorge dos Ilhéus* and *Os subterrâneos da liberdade*. While seldom gratuitous, sexual and scatological humor was not always satirically purposeful beyond the confines of documentary realism, however. Rather than lampooning a particular sector of society, some ribald episodes employed vulgarity simply as a means of mirroring a barbarian environment. *Terras do sem fim* was particularly rife with such incidents.

From the start of his literary career Amado likewise relied heavily on caricature to draw the social types that prevailed in his novels. Through the use of this device, characters often assumed cartoonlike proportions as the author comically exaggerated their salient physical or psychological-behavioral features at the expense of less notable traits. Physical caricature often took aim at the obesity of upper class characters or depicted characters of various classes as being eternally dressed in the same outlandish garb. The caricature of gestures was particularly associated with the orator, who was a ubiquitous figure in the novelist's works from the beginning. Psychological-behavioral caricature manifested itself in the speech mannerisms and obsessions of a number of minor personages. Macaronic speech, pet words and phrases, twangy voices, lisps, stutters, and the like were used to breathe life into many secondary characters who would otherwise have blended into the background. Caricature could be bitterly sarcastic, even sinister, with little humor, or lightheartedly comic with little vitriol. Usually it was somewhere between the two extremes.

In his *Análise estrutural de romances brasileiros,* Affonso Romano de Sant'Anna has called Amado's *Terras do sem fim* an example of what he designates as "counterideological narrative." "The myth of El Dorado is laid bare [demystified] by [the author's] narrating the struggles in the land of cacao. Within the book several visions coexist—one romantic, another realist, and still another fantastic—all with a single function: to denounce the utopian version [propounded by] the dominant ideology."[3] Indeed, most of Amado's early works—what we have here labeled *social realism*—seem to fit into this mold. The syntheses of such elements as document and lyricism, crudity and comedy, realism and caricature all had as their primary purpose the denunciation of a social, economic, and political reality that the novelist regarded as exploitative. To the extent that they were played off against one another, that no one of them was allowed to dominate the text, such elements served to depict that reality not only in its harshness but also in its many conflicts and complexities. It would take several attempts for the young Amado to achieve this goal.

Jubiabá: A Flawed Masterpiece

Jubiabá (1935) constitutes the first complete fruition of this scheme. Coming in the wake of *Cacau* (1933) and *Suor* (1934), it combines many of the traits of these works into a larger tapestry, one both urban and rural, picturesque yet politically committed, crudely realistic but also supremely lyrical. Gone is much of the awkwardness that had marked the earlier short novels. Instead of a succession of sketches bound together by a single common thread, *Jubiabá* is a complex interweaving of stories past and present recounting the meanderings of a black youth from a life of roguish adventures to adulthood and political activism. Though not as accomplished structurally as the later *Terras do sem fim* (1943) and some of the author's mature novels, it is, none-theless, a broader rendering of Bahian society, a richer fabric, of which the region's African cultural heritage and its vibrant folk culture were undeniably the warp and woof.

Scenes of Bahian *candomblé* (or *macumba,* as the author called it) punc-tuate the adventures of the protagonist, Antônio Balduíno. Amado treats such ritual sympathetically, integrating it into the story rather than presenting it as an exotic interlude designed merely to inject local color. Moreover, he consistently views African culture in a positive light. Antônio Balduíno is imbued by his mentor, Pai Jubiabá, with a sense of racial pride. It is from this *pai-de-santo* (*candomblé* priest) that he first learns of the history of oppression experienced by Brazilian blacks, and it is also because of him that Antônio comes to regard African religion and culture as a source of black identity and a means of resistance to that oppression. Likewise, Bahian folk tradition, a hy-brid of European and African culture, is blended into the novel's struc-ture. Not only do characters tell and sing stories about the exploits of bandits and popular heroes, but the author appropriates the ABC, a poetic form used to recount the epic feats of such heroes, to describe the final section of the novel, in which the protagonist, himself a writer of such verses, is apotheosized in an ABC many years later for his leadership in a triumphant dockworkers' strike and for his lifetime of struggle. Furthermore, the lyrics of sambas and such traditional Por-tuguese poems as the "Romance da nau catarineta" and the *cantigas de amigo* are carefully woven into the novelistic text.

As in the two previous works, the documentation of social problems is of paramount importance. There is no abatement of crude descrip-tions or frank exposé, nor is there an attenuation of the polemical tone of the earlier books. Like its predecessors, *Jubiabá* is a biting, tenden-tious denunciation of the injustices of an oppressive social system, whose victims were mostly poor and black. Yet because of the novelist's introduction and skillful manipulation of the elements of African and popular culture, it is also a polished and highly entertaining work of literature, marking the beginning of what one critic would call "the dialectic between naturalism . . . and popular poetry" characteristic of what he regards as the author's second phase.[4]

Indeed, the work was hailed as a masterpiece by some and came to be considered one of the high points of Amado's fiction. Antônio Cândido saw in it "a vastness theretofore unknown in [Brazilian] lit-erature,"[5] which he ascribed to the "poetry" of the work, its mystery and fascination with the sea. The Portuguese critic Adolfo Casais Monteiro emphasized the novel's use of the Bahian vernacular to create authentic dialogue along with its apposition of the sordid and the sublime, dubbing it an example of "lyrical realism."[6] And author Érico Veríssimo proclaimed the twenty-three-year-old creator of *Jubiabá* to be already one of the finest novelists in Brazil.[7] Yet others identified major flaws in the work: its simplistic division of characters into class-bound groupings; its occasional melodramatic excesses; the implausibility of its protagonist's sudden transformation from a hard-bitten scamp to a champion of the working classes and the consequent weakening of the novel's plot.

It was this last criticism that seemed to be the most serious. There was something of both the bildungsroman and the picaresque in the novel's largely episodic structure. Orphaned at an early age, Antônio Balduíno is raised by his aunt Luísa, a poor woman who prepares and sells typical Bahian dishes on the streets of Salvador not far from the *candomblé* of Pai Jubiabá. When Baldo, as he is nicknamed, is eleven, his aunt is committed to an insane asylum and he goes to live with Comendador Pereira, a wealthy Portuguese merchant who provides for his early education and whose daughter, Lindinalva, becomes the object of his infatuation. Falsely accused by a domestic of displaying indecent behavior toward the girl some four years later, Baldo runs away and becomes a beggar, joining a gang of waifs who roam the streets of the city. By the age of seventeen he is already a seasoned idler, composer of sambas, street fighter, and womanizer. Strong of body, he turns to boxing and becomes a champion, but quits the ring after suffering a humiliating defeat occasioned by his drunkenness, a reaction to the news of Lindinalva's engagement. After a brief wandering through the towns of the Bahian coastal region he signs on as a farm hand on a tobacco *fazenda* but is forced to flee some time later after stabbing the foreman in a fight. When next we see him, Baldo is a performer in a ragtag circus touring the towns of the Bahian interior. When the circus fails, he returns to Salvador, where he resumes the ways of a loafer at the age of twenty-seven. Lindinalva, in the meantime, has had a life of misery. Upon the bankruptcy of her father she is abandoned pregnant and penniless by her fiancé. Later orphaned, she is forced to turn to prostitution in order to support Gustavinho, her infant son. Broken and diseased, Lindinalva contacts Baldo and, on her deathbed, makes him promise to bring up the boy. In order to support him Baldo becomes a stevedore on the Salvador waterfront. When a strike breaks out soon thereafter he assumes a leadership role in the victorious struggle, which forever changes the direction of his life.

In a review of the novel written shortly after its publication Octávio Tarquínio de Souza pointed out the weakness of the protagonist's characterization, noting that "the end of the book, with the sudden, radical character transformation that Balduíno undergoes, betrays the novelist's presence and manifests the latter's desire, a desire to prove something."[8] Years later, Luís Costa Lima would echo this opinion: "In *Jubiabá*, Baldo's passage from a vagrant to an agitator is not convincing, for it relies on a sentimental cause, without there occurring any internal evolution in the character toward his new position as a revolutionary worker. . . . [It] is difficult to accept Baldo's activities as a striker as anything more than another adventure in his eventful life. The character's conversion to the work ethic as a result of the late Lindinalva's entrusting her son to him is not enough to lend coherence to the novel."[9]

Many of the same shortcomings would continue to plague the author in his two other "Bahian novels," *Mar morto* (1936; *Sea of Death*) and *Capitães da areia* (1937; *Captains of the Sands*). If *Jubiabá* was a masterpiece manqué owing to its factitious development of character and plot, both of the ensuing works would be found wanting by critics for what was regarded as their melodramatic proclivities and "oversentimentalization" of the wretched plight of the Bahian masses. Indeed, not until the publication of *Terras do sem fim* (*The Violent Land*) in 1943 would Amado lay such criticisms to rest. He had by then begun to master his craft as a prose fictionist and was now in full possession of the skills that would enable him to create the best of his later novels.

Terras do sem fim, or "The Epic of Cacao"

Any discussion by Brazilian literary critics of the merits and shortcomings of Amado's later fiction inevitably returns to a consideration of *Terras do sem fim* (1943; *The Violent Land*). So splendid is the novel's reputation that for years both the admirers and critics of the author's later fiction have regarded it as a touchstone by which to appraise the other works. Those who find in *Gabriela, Quincas,* and *Tereza Batista* the efflorescence of Amado's artistic genius point to *Terras* as the culmination of the novelist's early period and see the book as the immediate forerunner of the later, "mature" novels. Those who prefer the "old Amado" to the "new" one, however, tend to view *Terras do sem fim* as a benchmark of the writer's prose fiction to which the more recent works have all failed to measure up.

That the novel should retain this cachet after almost a half century of subsequent literary production by the author may or may not be an indication of the quality of later Amadian works. It is, however, strong evidence of the vast qualitative difference that separated *Terras do sem fim* from the writer's previous novels and attests to the high degree of literary expertise that the thirty-one-year-old Brazilian author had managed to acquire. Critics were almost unanimous in the opinion that *Terras* far outstripped its predecessors. "This is without a doubt [Amado's] greatest book," wrote Antônio Cândido, "much greater than the others, even *Jubiabá*. It is a great novel whose significance to our literature cannot at the moment be adequately gauged."[10] Another critic, Sérgio Milliet, agreed with this assessment, asserting that the Bahian had written "the most complete novel of his brilliant and productive career. We are in the presence not only of the masterpiece of Jorge Amado, but indeed of one of the great novels of our literature."[11] Still a third critic, Paulo Dantas, proclaimed the novelist to be "the great historian of the crude tales and simple men" of Brazil and saw in *Terras do sem fim* what he labeled "the epic of cacao growing."[12]

But if *Terras* was indeed a qualitative improvement over the author's previous works, what then were the specific ways in which it surpassed its immediate predecessors? The words of Antônio Cândido suggest some of the answers:

Frankly speaking, in *Mar morto* Mr. Jorge Amado loses his footing and plunges into pure poetry. The document disappears before the lyrical impetus, and the novel almost becomes a poem.

In *Capitães da areia* documentary reasserts itself. The author tries to strike a balance between the two tendencies, but produces a book appreciably inferior to the two preceding ones.

In *Terras do sem fim* we arrive at a kind of solution to the aforementioned dialectical movement: we arrive, so to speak, at the esthetic formula of Mr. Jorge Amado. Document and poetry are harmoniously blended by way of the historical novel.[13]

Indeed, the superiority of *Terras* to the author's other works lies to a considerable extent in the harmonious fusion of "document" and "poetry." In a prefatory note to *Cacau* (1933) Amado had announced his intention "to recount in this book, with a *minimum of literature* and a maximum of honesty, the lives of the workers on the cacao *fazendas* of southern Bahia," ending with the rhetorical question, "Is it then a proletarian novel?" (italics mine). Whatever the appropriateness or inappropriateness of the term *proletarian* here, the writer had indeed succeeded in this series of loosely intertwined sketches and in its successor, *Suor,* in assembling a kind of slice-of-life account of the woes of the dispossessed of urban and rural Bahia. But he had fallen short of producing a coherent novel. *Jubiabá* had attained this goal precisely because it had reintegrated "literature" into the mix, enhancing document with the poetry of African and popular culture and thus producing a richer, more intricate texture. Yet it too suffered from a lack of disciplined structuring, an ailment of which the protagonist's abrupt ideological awakening was but a single symptom. *Mar morto* and *Capitães da areia* would seek to remedy this imperfection, as Cândido observes, but would fall prey to other excesses. Not until *Terras,* then, would the solution be found.

Like its three immediate predecessors, *Terras do sem fim* incorporates extensive lyrical passages into the novelistic text. But while the Bahian novels, located primarily in Salvador, sing of the mysteries of *candomblé* and of the ever-present sea, *Terras* poeticizes the dark tropical forests of the southern region, which stubbornly resisted the advance of the cacao plantations with their golden fruit. What is more, the novel is underlaid with allusions to classical myth and larded with biblical overtones. The ship ferrying some of the characters to the port of Ilhéus at the beginning of the book is strongly reminiscent of the boat of Charon, as Affonso Romano de Sant'Anna has noted.[14] Cacao barons are styled in much the same manner as Old Testament patriarchs, and episodes such as Dr. Jessé's tree-planting ceremony and the destruction of the forest sanctuary of a witch doctor named Jeremias are virtual parodies of biblical events.[15]

Cândido's identification of the work as a historical novel, however, goes beyond the assertion that it attains a felicitous mixture of document and poetry. Set amid the land wars of the cacao-growing region of Bahia around the time of the author's birth, *Terras do sem fim* is a historical novel in much the same sense as Steinbeck's *Grapes of Wrath.* Like the latter, it is a novel of social consciousness that attempts to fuse individual with collective history, and penetrating analysis of human psychology and behavior with social portraiture and exposé. It too seeks to chronicle the times, to chart the peculiar historical and economic coordinates of a specific period by showing the effect that

historical and economic forces exercise on characters representing particular social classes. While Steinbeck employs so-called interchapters
to supply the narrative with social and historical information that il-
luminates the story, Amado supplements the *récit* of *Terras* with the
editorials and news accounts of fictitious local dailies, with the tales of
frontier storytellers, and with the occasional verses of the blind trou-
badours who sang the epic of cacao. Like Steinbeck's novel, *Terras* de-
scribes both the heroic and the ignominious, the sordid and the
sublime. Although it does not hesitate to unmask social injustice wherever it finds it, the novel, unlike its Amadian predecessors, avoids a
strict separation of good and evil along class lines.

It was this attitude of detachment, of dispassionate narration coupled with a heightened concern for probing his characters' thoughts
and motivations that constitutes one of the major innovations of Amado's *Terras do sem fim*. He makes no secret of his sympathy for the
novel's underdogs. But victims are not confined to the lower strata of
society. All, in one way or another, are shown to be products of their
particular circumstances; haves as well as have-nots are victimized by
the excesses spawned by cacao. More often than not, victims and vic-
timizers are one and the same. Such is the case of Damião, a hired
gunman famed for his marksmanship and reputation as a killer. Despite that image, he is also one of the gentlest of human beings, an
innocent pawn whose loyalty and naïveté prevent him from questioning the morality of the Colonel's orders to kill. But one day when he
is called upon by his employer to eliminate an enemy in a routine
ambush, it occurs to him that the consequences of his actions are evil
and that he and he alone must decide what is right and wrong. He is
seized by sudden compassion for the family of his intended victim. In
one of the finest passages of the novel Damião's internal conflicts, his
misgivings and incipient doubts, become the subject of a lengthy, indirect interior monologue that leads him to fail in his assignment and
lose all touch with reality. Other characters, such as the adventurer
João Magalhães, lawyer Virgílio Cabral, and a kept woman named Margot, likewise play the dual role of victim and victimizer to varying
degrees, yet none with quite the drama and anguish of Damião.

Perhaps the best example of the author's newfound objectivity,
though, lies in his characterization of the *coronéis* (colonels, or large
planters; singular: *coronel*), for whom he displays an uneasy combination of sympathy and revulsion. Unlike Col. Manuel Misael de Sousa
Teles of *Cacau,* whom the novelist treats with unalloyed scorn, the

planters of *Terras* are awe-inspiring figures, drawn larger than life in
the manner of epic or biblical heroes. It is they who make and enforce
the law of the frontier, who are the patriarchs of the region, directing
its future and the lives of its inhabitants. Indeed, Sinhô Badaró and
Col. Horácio da Silveira, the two most powerful political chieftains of
the area, "are among the novelist's most acute psychological studies,"
as Fred P. Ellison observed in his 1954 monograph on northeastern
Brazilian novelists.[16] Both are self-made men who are crude in their
ways. The former is an imposing figure. Almost two meters tall with
a long black beard down to his chest, he has the nightly custom of
having the Bible opened at random and passages read to him so that
he may interpret them as prophecies by which to guide his affairs. The
latter is no less striking in his appearance and behavior. With a dour
countenance scarred by smallpox and enormous calloused hands from
his early days as a whip-wielding muledriver, he is rumored to have
brutally murdered those who have dared to mock him or stand in his
way. It is said that he flogged his first wife to death after finding her
in bed with another man. He is without scruples, and unlike Sinhô
Badaró, who regards murdering his adversaries as a kind of distasteful
necessity, he seems to derive no small amount of pleasure from inflict-
ing pain upon others. Yet he is also pictured as a kind of foolish clown
in one episode, dressed for bed in his nightshirt embroidered with
small red flowers. Despite such characterizations, however, there is also
something awesome, even noble about his demeanor and strength of
mind, an epic grandeur that serves to enlarge rather than diminish him
in the reader's eyes.

This multifaceted view of the *coronel* presented in *Terras do sem fim*
has been laid to the author's genuine admiration for the type in real
life. "These were heroic men he had known himself," states Ellison.
"His own father was a cacao planter."[17] Certainly, Amado's personal
experience, his childhood amid the violence and boomtown mentality
of the Bahian frontier, played an important role in such characterizations. As an infant he himself had almost been the victim of one of the
notorious ambushes. As a boy he had witnessed his father's participa-
tion in the Sequeiro Grande cacao wars and had looked on as one *coronel*
was tried for his alleged crimes in the land disputes, an episode that
would serve as a basis for the trial of Col. Horácio in the present novel.
But he had also been an eyewitness to many of the Promethean exploits
of such men: the clearing of vast tracts of land, the cutting of roads
through the tropical wilderness, the erecting of towns such as Ferradas

and Tabocas (Itabuna). And he had seen the fierce loyalty accorded such titans by the populace, comparable only to that rendered by vassals to a feudal overlord. Little wonder, then, that he pictures the *coronel* in this almost paradoxical way, endowing him with the humanity and heroic stature that the Marxist in him would later deny the money-grubbing cacao exporters of *São Jorge dos Ilhéus*.

Greater objectivity is likewise attained in *Terras* by the novelist's intertwining of multiple protagonists and subplots into the text. *Jubiabá* and *Mar morto* largely focus on the adventures of single heroes—Antônio Balduíno and Guma—and *Capitães da areia*, although to some extent it follows the lives of the individual members of the band, is primarily the story of Pedro Bala. *Terras do sem fim*, however, narrates several ongoing stories, alternating the adventures of the two patriarchs and their immediate families with those of a number of other primary and secondary figures. We witness the frustrations of the polished Ester, who, horrified by the barbarous lifestyle of the region and the crudity of her husband, Horácio, seeks affection in the arms of her husband's attorney, the handsome Virgílio Cabral. We are told of the latter's liaison with Margot, who later becomes the mistress of Juca Badaró, the dissolute younger brother of Sinhô. And we accompany the romance of the tomboyish Don'Ana Badaró, the patriarch's daughter, with João Magalhães, a status-seeking adventurer. Don'Ana is particularly well developed as a character and serves as the paradigm for several of the author's later strong female personages. There is also the story of Raimunda, an illegitimate mulatto girl raised in the shadow of Don'Ana, whose strong-mindedness and diligence are exceeded only by her bitterness toward one and all. And in one of the most lyrical sequences in the novel we are told the story of the three sisters—Maria, Lúcia, and Violeta—who end up working as prostitutes in the same brothel through no fault of their own. The introduction of such subplots and episodes invests the text with greater breadth and pluralism as the perspectives of the two opposing landowners—in reality but a single monolithic worldview—are contrasted with and often undercut by those of their relatives and followers. Ego is played off against ego; competing interests serve to correct one another. There is a constant back-and-forth movement, which makes for greater fluidity and a more intricate plot structure. Thus *Terras* provides a less univocal, more balanced, and ultimately much more satisfying interpretation of the events it recounts.

Amado does not retreat here from his earlier portrayals of the exploitation of farmworkers and their families. In *Terras do sem fim,* as always, it is the poor and the blacks who receive the most inhumane treatment from the ruling classes. But more than ever their tragedies are submerged in the larger pattern of greed and brutality that infects the entire social gamut. All are consumed by the obsessive quest for cacao. Nor does the novel shy away from the earthiness and profanity of the earlier books. If anything, their incidence proliferates, but increasingly they are coupled with irony or broad humor. Accordingly, it would be a mistake to view the work as a wholesale break with earlier Amadian patterns. Indeed, in many ways it is an intensification of the traits displayed in the three Bahian novels, buttressed by the author's greater maturity and sure-footedness. To have written this "epic of cacao," Amado had to sharpen his literary tools and refine his understanding of history and the human soul, forsaking the constraints imposed by a narrow ideological view. Part of the work's uniqueness stems from the fact that it would be some years before he would again reap the fruits of this lesson.

Chapter Three
Gabriela, cravo e canela:
A Chronicle of Cacao, Love, and Liberation

The "New" Jorge Amado: Humor, Irony, and Satire

The publication of *Gabriela, cravo e canela* (*Gabriela, Clove and Cinnamon*) in 1958 led many critics to postulate the existence of a new, more mature Amado. To be sure, there were those who regarded the novel as ideological heresy. But the majority of Brazilian critics deemed it a welcome change from the dogmatism of many of the author's previous works, identifying humor and irony as its chief distinctive ingredients and labeling the latter with such adjectives as "picaresque," "playful," and "irreverent."

Not that humor and irony were lacking in Amado's earlier fiction. Indeed, caricature, as we noted previously, was a mainstay of the author's style from the very beginning. So too were such elements as sexual and scatological humor, hyperbolic folk anecdotes, class satire, pranks, and sarcasm. Yet with *Gabriela* there is a marked intensification of the use of comic and ironic techniques, primarily for satirical purposes. Not only are there heavier doses of the aforementioned devices, but humor, which performed an essentially ancillary function in many of the early books, is now all-pervasive. It assumes a major part in the development of character and plot. Moreover, it is now usually the basis of novelistic tone; virtually everything is to some degree funny, though seldom without satirical relevance. If in the earlier novels humor often took the form of comic-relief episodes digressing from the central plot line, it is now better assimilated into the texture of the work, more thoroughly integrated into its narrative structure.

What is more, broad comic devices are frequently joined here by more refined modes of humor, such as irony and verbal wit. Irony is used particularly to underscore the incongruities of dogmatic belief and to proclaim the relativity of truth. Comic exaggeration, long cultivated by Amado, is counterpoised with such ironic techniques as euphemism, circumlocution, antiphrasis, understatement, and transferred epithets, which lend greater subtlety, depth, and complexity to the novelist's prose. This is especially significant for characterization. To be sure, Amado does not cease to depict characters along class lines; he still tends to favor the oppressed masses and condemn their exploiters. But characters are no longer treated monolithically. Rather, they are drawn with greater ironic distance, a leveling effect being achieved in the process. Instead of viewing the rich as evil and the poor as morally superior, he tends to poke fun at the shortcomings of both groups with a mixture of sympathy and detachment. This tendency, first observed in the earlier *Terras,* is intensified here by the introduction of humorous and ironic tongue-in-cheek phrasings. Thus, in *Gabriela* pompous hypocrites such as Padre Basílio Cerqueira and Dr. Argileu Palmeira are described with antiphrastic epithets that are comically incongruous, not deprecatory. The former, a Catholic cleric famed for his considerable landholdings and growing number of progeny, is referred to on several occasions as "the holy man" or "the saint" (*Gabriela,* 26, 28). Similarly, the latter receives such comically ironic titles as "the inspired bard" (*Gabriela,* 305), "the illustrious inhabitant of Parnassus" (*Gabriela,* 306), and "the eminent" (*Gabriela,* 316)—labels that obliquely affirm his literary mediocrity while seemingly belying it. Wordplay, alliteration, zeugmatic constructions, and the like, while occasionally used for satirical purposes, primarily serve to enhance the overall ludic character of the author's prose.

Closely related to irony is the novelist's cultivation in *Gabriela* of several types of incongruous juxtaposition. Easily the most elaborate description of such an assemblage is the Nativity scene of the Dos Reis sisters (*Gabriela,* 73–80). Though any irreverence on the sisters' part is unwitting, alongside the figures of Mary, Joseph, and others traditionally linked to the holiest of Christian scenes there appears "the radiant fleshiness of half-naked movie stars" (*Gabriela,* 76). Replacing the weather-beaten image of Melchior, one of the Magi, is a recent (that is, 1925) photograph of the sultan of Morocco (*Gabriela,* 77).

There was Santos Dumont standing beside one of his early aeroplanes, wearing a sporty hat and a rather sad look on his face. Near him, on the right slope of a hill, was Herod conversing with Pilate. Further on, stood heroes of the war: King George V of England, the Kaiser, Marshal Joffre, Lloyd George, Poincaré, Czar Nicholas. On the left-hand slope, Eleonora Duse stood out, a crown on her head, her arms bare. Near her were Rui Barbosa, J. J. Seabra, Lucien Guitry, Victor Hugo, Dom Pedro II, Emílio de Menezes, the Baron of Rio Branco, Zola and Dreyfyus, the poet Castro Alves, and the bandit Antônio Silvino. . . .

In the last few years, the number of movie stars—the chief contribution of the pupils at the parochial girls' school—had greatly increased. William Farnum, Eddie Polo, Lia de Putti, Rudolph Valentino, Charlie Chaplin, Lillian Gish, Ramon Novarro, and William S. Hart threatened to dominate the roads leading to the hillsides. Even Vladimir Ilyich Lenin, the feared leader of the Bolshevik revolution, was there. (*Gabriela*, 77–78)

Gabriela had helped Quinquina and Florzinha with their final preparations. She had cut out pictures and glued them on pasteboard and she had made artificial flowers. At Nacib's uncle's house, she found some magazines from Syria, and this is how several Muslims, pashas, and oriental sultans turned up in the democratic tableau, to the delight of João Fulgêncio, Nhô Galo, and Felipe the cobbler. Joaquim had built some hydroplanes out of cardboard and hung them over the stable. They were this year's novelty. (*Gabriela*, 375)

Such a gallimaufry combines basic descriptive technique with one of enumeration. The resulting catalogue seems, consequently, to provide not only an index to the sui generis tableau but also, in microcosm, to Ilhéus, Bahia, Brazil, and the world itself. Here, in the crèche, all types are tolerated and, while such an attitude may stem at bottom from the spinsters' naïveté, no one is denied his or her place in the sun.

A similar ironic leveling effect is found in many of the book's lengthy chapter and section titles and in its use of humorous catalogue-like enumerations, both of which make their first appearance in *Gabriela*. The first of these devices is treated in greater detail in the next section of this chapter. For purposes of the present discussion, suffice it to say that both devices, in addition to their obvious parodic functions, often serve to homogenize seemingly incompatible elements, as if by placing them together the novelist were seeking to minimize their incongruities. Like the enumerative, archaizing chapter and section titles, textual lists are reminiscent of those found in many of the descriptive treatises, dialogues, and poems of sixteenth- and seventeenth-century Brazil. Amado's lists, however, replace the naive colonial *ufanismo* (excessive patriotic bragging) over the country's boundless natural resources with tongue-in-cheek praise for both the best and the worst traditions of the old order as well as for the multifarious, but often dubious, wonders bestowed on the cacao-growing region by the long-awaited advent of material progress.

One such piece of enumerative patchwork, appearing on the first page of chapter one (*Gabriela*, 25), relates some of the diverse manifestations of this newfound wealth. From greater educational opportunities to larger houses, costlier furniture, better-stocked retail shops and burgeoning commerce, it quickly shades into such telling growth indicators as booming night clubs, increased drinking and gambling, and a mounting influx of females—"in short, progress, the civilization that everyone talked about." By thus mingling these ostensibly incompatible elements under the irreproachable umbrella of progress, the novelist jokingly gives the impression that he is placing his stamp of approval on whatever changes may flow from the capitalist cornucopia, irrespective of their possible deleterious social effects. A similarly facetious collocation appears in a discussion of how quickly newcomers to the region manage to assimilate the established ways of long-time residents. "They arrived, and in a short time they were the best of ilheenses, true native sons, planting fields, setting up stores and markets, opening roads, killing people, gambling in the cabarets, drinking in the bars, building towns that mushroomed, clearing the threatening forest, winning and losing money, feeling as native as the oldest ilheenses, sons of the families from before the coming of cacao" (*Gabriela*, 56). The satirical force of these two examples lies first and foremost in their ironic, mock-epic homogenization of customs and values not normally lumped together. Making use of the comic principle of deceived expectations, they likewise resemble the aforementioned ironic techniques to the extent that they too relativize the novelistic discourse by saying one thing and meaning another.

Irony and incongruous juxtaposition in the "new" Amado also give rise to other textual practices that will be more fully developed in later works. The "double perspective" of *Quincas* and *Comandante,* the use of roman à clef characters in *Dona Flor,* and the introduction of the Afro-Bahian supernatural in *Dona Flor, Tereza,* and other novels are explored in subsequent chapters. The novelist's recourse to parodic techniques in several of his mature works merits special attention. In *Quincas* it will take the form of a pastiche of the biblical Passion; in *Dona Flor* it will lead to a burlesquing of recipes and menus. And in *Tereza* Amado will mock the generic features of the *literatura de cordel,* or popular verse chapbook. It is in *Gabriela,* however, that the novelist first makes substantial use of the satirical device by parodying the Renaissance chronicles of discovery and exploration.

Chronicle Parody

The subtitle of *Gabriela, cravo e canela,* unfortunately omitted in the
English translation, reads, "Crônica de uma cidade do interior"
(Chronicle of an interior town), as if to alert the reader to the author's
parodic intentions. These are subsequently made manifest in a series of
textual devices openly evoking the literature of times past, many of
them appropriated specifically from the Portuguese *crônicas* of discovery
and exploration of the sixteenth and seventeenth centuries.[1]

The most obvious of such borrowings are the archaizing, sesquipedalian
chapter and section titles used to divide the novel. Utilizing such introductory expressions as *de como* (of how), *onde* (wherein), and *do/da* (of the),
along with the connectives *e* (and) and *com* (with), these headings constitute
camp, mock-heroic reminders of bygone literary traditions, appealing as
they do to a hyperbolic, verbose esthetic long since outmoded. Hence their
connections to both comical overstatement and ironic understatement.
They are often enumerative in the manner of an index or catalogue, thus
resembling the humorous lists that appear in the text itself. This is particularly true of the lengthy rubrics introducing the novel's two parts, the
first of which reads as follows:

Adventures and Misadventures of a Good Brazilian (Born in Syria) in the Town
of Ilhéus, in 1925, When Cacao Flourished and Progress Reigned—With
Love Affairs, Murders, Banquets, Crèches, Various Stories for All Tastes, a
Remote and Glorious Past of Lordly Aristocrats and Rogues, a Recent Past of
Wealthy Planters and Notorious Hoodlums, with Loneliness and Sighs, De-
sire, Vengeance, Hatred, with Rain and Sun and Moonlight, Inflexible Laws,
Political Maneuvers, the Controversial Issue of the Sandbar, along with a Pres-
tidigitator, a Dancer, a Miracle, and Other Wonders; or, A Brazilian from
Araby (*Gabriela,* 21)

In terms of wordiness and historical pretension, this title is not unlike
those used, for example, by the sixteenth-century Portuguese chronicler João de Barros in his monumental *Décadas da Asia* (1552–63):

How, once Pedro Alvares had parted, he met a storm in the vicinity of Cape
Verde; and, continuing on his route, discovered the great land that we commonly call Brazil, to which he gave the name Santa Cruz, and how, before
arriving in Mozambique, he met another storm in which he lost four ships.
(*Década* 1.2.2)

How, after Vasco da Gama made peace with the Sheik of Mozambique, who promised him a pilot to guide him to India, the peace was broken; and of what happened subsequently. (*Década* 1.4.7)

In both the Barros and Amadian examples, the enumerative character of the title eliminates in advance much of the suspense that the history or story might have possessed. While this was perfectly appropriate to the chronicle genre, with its historiographical pretensions, it is largely out of character for the novel and is attributable rather to the author's desire to exempt his work from the normal conventions of novel reading by facetiously associating it with those of a naive, outmoded genre. Many of the shorter, yet still wordy, chapter and subchapter titles likewise parody the older tradition: "Wherein Appears Mundinho Falcão, an Important Character, Looking at Ilhéus Through Binoculars" (*Gabriela*, 60); "Of How Mrs. Saad Became Involved in Politics, Violating Her Husband's Traditional Neutrality, and of the Daring and Dangerous Steps of This Lady of High Society During Her Night of Adventure" (*Gabriela*, 349); "Of How the Arab Nacib Broke the Ancient Law and Resigned from the Illustrious Order of St. Cornelius, or Of How Mrs. Saad Became Gabriela Again" (*Gabriela*, 391).

The humorous textual lists, as we noted in the preceding section, are also part of the chronicle tradition. Like the titles themselves, they are reminiscent of the chronicler's effort to catalogue the divers wonders of the exotic, newly discovered lands: the topography, the flora, the fauna, the peoples, and their strange customs. Thus the narrator of *Gabriela*, as if he were a bedazzled eyewitness to such a discovery, heaps enumeration upon enumeration in an almost feverish attempt to inventory the folkways and newfound progress of this interior town. Admittedly, not all of the lists reflect the author's penchant for ironic, incongruous juxtaposition, like those discussed above. Some merely serve the purpose of adding to the general pattern of prolixity and stylistic exuberance that marks *Gabriela* and many of the later novels. But whether they perform an ironic leveling function by seeking to homogenize heteroclite elements or simply help to generate a climate and syntactical rhythms associated with excess, such textual catalogues are undeniably parodic to the degree that they convey not only the original voice of the appropriated text, but also, perhaps more importantly, the secondary voice of the appropriating novelist, often facetiously at variance with the former.

The Renaissance chronicle of discovery and exploration, though primarily oriented toward observation and description of the empirical world, retained something of the older medieval chronicle in that it also sometimes included elements of the fantastic, or supernatural. It likewise permitted the incorporation of other genres and, therefore, frequently seemed to have an amorphous structure. While the chroniclers often employed such expressions as "the complete truth," "the true history," and "a faithful and complete account" to arrogate total veracity to their works, many such chronicles were anything but objective in their reporting, particularly insofar as they failed to distinguish between real and magical occurrences. In *Gabriela* Amado does indeed combine the supernatural with the natural, though not to the degree that he will in *Pastores, Dona Flor, Tereza,* and other later works. The ritual and magic of *candomblé* are seen primarily in the subchapter entitled "Of the Comrade on the Battlefield" (*Gabriela,* 432–37) near the end of the novel. There is, to be sure, a certain homogenizing of the empirical and the magical. There is also some irony in the fact that the Afro-Bahian supernatural is portrayed here as more "real" than its Christian counterpart. But as in several of the earlier works, Afro-Bahian religious elements are not yet fully integrated into the plot structure.

Not so the introductory poems. As in the sixteenth- and seventeenth-century chronicles, poetic interludes are freely introduced into the prose narrative of *Gabriela* in much the same manner as the epigraphs that precede them. Some are penned in a mock-heroic or mock-exotic style, which serves to strengthen their connection with the novelist's parody of the chronicle tradition. (Greater attention is given to introductory poems in the final section of this chapter.)

Other elements might be regarded as forming part of the genre parody. The epigraphs themselves certainly belong to an earlier literary tradition no longer in vogue, although they do not necessarily derive from the chronicle per se. The prominence of spices such as clove and cinnamon likewise brings to mind the exotic cargoes of many a Renaissance caravel and galleon. And the return to Ilhéus of southerner Mundinho Falcão, who spies the city through binoculars while perched on the deck of an arriving ship, is not unlike that of Columbus in his triumphant second voyage to the Indies. Yet, it remains unclear just to what extent such elements were actually intended to participate in the parody.

It might well be objected that the imitation and comic exaggeration in *Gabriela* of the various features of the *crônica* does not go beyond playful stylization.[2] Yet unless one takes the view that parody must needs imply total rejection of the parodied genre or style, the novelist's creation and maintenance of ironic distance between himself and the appropriated literary conventions would seem to be enough to qualify the novel as a parodic text. Indeed, his often ludicrous imitation of some of the chronicle's most salient characteristics, while avoiding ridicule, usually involves, as we have seen, the establishment of a "double-voiced" discourse in which his own esthetic values are playfully at odds with those of the parodied style. One could likewise argue that the parody in *Gabriela* is only partial, as would indeed seem to be the case in several subsequent Amadian novels. But this would not necessarily diminish its intended effects.

What, then, are these effects? Earlier, we observed that one of them stems from the novelist's attempt to exempt the book from the usual conventions of novel reading that we, as readers, impose on a fictional text. By calling his work a chronicle and carefully weaving into it several of the latter's most notable generic trappings, he seeks to free himself from having to develop a tight-knit plot, create suspense, and analyze characters' psychological motivations, among other things. And whereas such characteristically Amadian traits as prolixity, desultoriness, lyricism, and a flair for the fantastic are often deemed anathema by the standards of the modern novel, they are perfectly acceptable to the *crônica,* where they thrive in its hybrid climate of fact and fiction. The novelist's simultaneous identification with and burlesquing of the conventions of this camp, timeworn genre, then, afford him the luxury of writing a novel that breaks many of the rules.

This is not to say, however, that he imitates the *crônica* merely in an effort to turn his own traditional stylistic vices into virtues. Both the medieval and Renaissance chronicles may rightfully be regarded as forerunners not only of modern historiography but also of the historical novel, a subgenre that Amado had cultivated earlier in *Terras do sem fim, São Jorge dos Ilhéus,* and *Os subterrâneos da liberdade.* What is more, since it chronologically bridged the gap between the waning of feudalism and the appearance of early capitalism, the *crônica* was the perfect vehicle through which to portray a similar economic, political, and social transition taking place on the Brazilian frontier. But this time, instead of singing the epic of cacao, Amado chooses to describe the momentous changes from a coign of vantage that would allow him to depict characters in a mock-heroic fashion, framing their deeds and misdeeds ironically as if to negate the absoluteness of their moral value. By parodying an older genre that ludicrously claimed to tell the whole truth, he was, on the one hand, acknowledging the ultimate subjectivity of all historical and novelistic discourse while, on the other, ironically, achieving greater detachment than he had in any of his earlier fiction.

Escape from the Tower: Female Characters and Their Sociopolitical Symbolism

The prominence of female characters in *Gabriela, cravo e canela* has attracted the attention of several scholars since the book was first published in 1958. One critic has analyzed the relationship between the novelist's use of introductory poems and his portrayal of the various heroines' strivings for greater personal freedom in an evolving socioeconomic milieu.[3] Another has observed the book's depiction of the "psychological imprisonment suffered by women" in traditional Brazilian society.[4] A third has detected in the novel what he regards as contrapuntal, though complementary, "feminine" and "masculine" structures.[5] And finally, a fourth critic has used it to examine the role alternatives available to Brazilian women in this century as opposed to last.[6] But no one, to my knowledge, has yet addressed *Gabriela* as the feminist statement that I believe it seeks to be.[7] The present section will attempt to do so by relating Amado's subversion of traditional female literary stereotypes—as well as his deliberate modification of his own alternative types through irony and greater individualization—to his advocacy of social and political liberation, of which greater freedom of choice for women appears to be an important component.

Females in literature and anthropology have frequently been stereotyped into such categories as siren, mother, and damsel. More often than not, they have been characterized as passive, fickle, illogical, mysterious, and deceitful, if not also idealized or regarded as inherently evil. Such images tend necessarily to reflect the distortions, biases, and oversimplifications of a traditional male viewpoint, given the longstanding predominance of men in these fields. And although in Latin America some power and prestige have traditionally been attached to the figure of the matriarch, in reality her prerogatives have often been severely circumscribed, if allowed to exist at all, by an overwhelmingly patriarchal society.

It is perhaps significant that in *Gabriela* Amado includes no motherly figure comfortable in her role as powerful matriarch of a family or grande dame of an entire town. Indeed, the role of mother in the tra-

ditional patriarchal society of Ilhéus and the cacao-growing region of
southern Bahia would appear to be no stronger or less passive than the
other traditional roles assumed by the novel's female characters. Judg-
ing by the various heroines of *Gabriela,* it might be claimed that the
ilheense woman of 1925 possessed little real power or control over her
own life as long as she remained in her "proper" place, as defined by
the dictates of the patriarchal system. Ilhéus was a man's world, and a
woman—be she mother, daughter, sister, wife, or paramour—was expected to be submissive to her "rightful lord and master."

"A woman's place is in the home, taking care of the children and
the house," (*Gabriela,* 89) ran the time-honored view. Or, as one tra-
ditionalist put it, "the home is the fortress of the virtuous woman"
(*Gabriela,* 157). "Young women are supposed to prepare for marriage
by learning how to sew, play the piano and run the kitchen" (*Gabriela,*
89). Never mind that their brothers were sent to college or high school
in the state capital of Salvador and were allowed to live as they pleased,
unsupervised, and supplied with generous monthly stipends to support
them. Young women could not possibly aspire to the same treatment,
for it was not considered proper for an adolescent female to live apart
from her family or even to continue her education.

All that a girl had of her own was that brief period of adolescence. The parties
at the Progress Club, a few insignificant flirtations, the exchanging of love
letters, stolen kisses at the movie matinees, at times more passionate ones at
the garden gate. Her father would arrive one day with a friend. The flirtation
was over; now she was engaged. Even if she objected, he would force her into
it. Once in a while a girl married her boyfriend, when her parents liked him
too. But that didn't change the situation at all. Whether he was a husband
handpicked by her father or a bridegroom chosen by fate, it was all the same.
Once she was married, it made no difference. He was her owner, her lord and
master; he dictated the laws and was to be obeyed and respected. He had all
the rights, she the duties. She was the guardian of the family honor, of her
husband's name, the one responsible for the house and the children. (*Gabriela,*
278).[8]

Nor were things any better for the "not-so-virtuous" female. An
outgrowth of the double sexual standard, prostitution thrived. So did
concubinage. According to the conventional wisdom, some women had
to be sacrificed to protect the virtue of others. Thus, prostitutes and
concubines served the "noble" purpose of safeguarding the wives and

daughters of Ilhéus from the "insatiable" male libido.[9] But this meant that they, too, were at the mercy of male domination and, in the case of the concubine, that she was often regarded as private property and, like the wife or daughter, must lead a secluded existence.

Thus, as in the "princess-held-captive-in-a-tower" motif of many a medieval tale, only by escaping her confinement could the *ilheense* woman hope to attain a measure of freedom and begin to exercise some dominion over her circumstances.[10] But such escape without the aid and consent of the proper male companion (Prince Charming?) was strictly barred by convention, while with it there was frequently no escape at all, but merely an exchange of one type of confinement for another. The traditional female stereotypes of virtue—and, for that matter, also those of vice—each possessed a corollary image picturing the punishment of those who dared to deviate from the prescribed norm.[11] So, too, any transgression of the sex roles deemed proper for a particular class of *ilheense* female would inevitably lead to severe punishment.

Chronologically, the first of the novel's female characters to attempt to escape her "towered" existence is the aristocratic, nineteenth-century maiden, Ofenísia d'Ávila, whose languorous imprisonment and pleas for deliverance introduce the first chapter (*Gabriela,* 23–24). Prevented by her brother, Luís Antônio, from becoming the mistress of the Brazilian emperor, Dom Pedro II, whom she has met while he is in Bahia, Ofenísia rebels. She refuses to have anything to do with the wealthy marriage prospects arranged for her, choosing instead to die a virgin, locked away in the family mansion (*Gabriela,* 45–48, 128). Her tormented thoughts are reproduced in the chapter's poetic epigraph:

> I want no count, no baron,
> I want no sugar planter,
>
> . . . .
>
> All that I want is the beard,
> So black, of the Emperor!
> My brother, Luís Antônio,
> Of the illustrious house of Ávila,
> Listen, oh my brother:
> If I cannot be the mistress
> Of His Highness the Emperor,
> Then I shall die in this hammock
> Of languor.
>
> (*Gabriela,* 24)

Passive though she is in her revolt against male domination (she is virtually treated as a child by her brother), Ofenísia is remembered not as a submissive victim but as an unyielding martyr to the cause of women's emancipation. Nor is she held up by any but the most reactionary of modern *ilheense* citizens as an example of one who has been justly penalized for having overstepped the bounds of decorum. Though a mere legend in the town's collective memory, she becomes a source of inspiration—a patron saint of sorts—to the twentieth-century *ilheense* women in their rebellion against the stifling restrictions imposed on them by tradition. If during her lifetime she was unsuccessful in her efforts to gain release from her palatial prison, she is, nonetheless, triumphant in death as a symbol of nonconformity and a model of female determination and defiance. Thus, despite her captivity, Ofenísia is depicted as something more than the traditionally helpless damsel in distress.[12] The tragic case of Dona Sinhazinha Guedes Mendonça, a distant descendant of Ofenísia, is a chapter from the current history of Ilhéus. Trapped in an unhappy marriage to a boorish, domineering planter twenty years her senior, over the years she attempts to conceal her romantic frustrations by indulging in frills and church activities. Because of her reputation as a paragon of Christian virtue and a pillar of local society, it comes as a shock to the entire community when she is suddenly caught in flagrante delicto and murdered along with her young lover by the irate husband, Col. Jesuíno (*Gabriela,* 17, 124–37).

The latter's speedy acquittal is a foregone conclusion. No one, man or woman, steps forward to defend the slain adulteress; praise for her husband's action is nearly as unanimous as is condemnation of her infidelity. According to an unwritten *ilheense* law, "the honor of a deceived husband could be cleansed only by blood. . . . There was no punishment known for an unfaithful wife other than violent death" (*Gabriela,* 126).[13] No jury in Ilhéus had ever brought in a verdict of guilty against a man accused of killing his unfaithful wife and her lover. Thus, the town is even more greatly astonished when in the end Col. Jesuíno Mendonça is convicted of murder and sentenced to prison (*Gabriela,* 453).

Although hers is an ill-fated rebellion, Sinhazinha, like Ofenísia, is at least partially vindicated in death. Slowly, the townspeople of Ilhéus come to regard her punishment as excessive and begin to view her desperate behavior with tolerant, albeit disapproving, comprehension. Was she alone culpable for the "indiscretion"? Or, as one character suggests, why not blame "certain husbands who ignored their wives, treated them like servants, while giving everything—jewels and perfumes, expensive dresses and luxury items—to the prostitutes that they supported or to the *mulata* mistresses whom they set up in houses?" (*Gabriela*, 133). Indeed, like her unfortunate ancestor, Sinhazinha eventually assumes the role of a sacrificial victim, though certainly an unconventional one. She is not a martyr, for no one condones her actions. Nonetheless, she is perceived as a type of scapegoat, as "the one who had to die" so that future generations of *ilheense* women might be spared from the barbarous practice of sanctioned uxoricide.[14]

Ironically, the most secluded of the novel's female characters is not the wife, sister, or daughter of a planter, but Col. Coriolano Ribeiro's kept mistress, Glória. Perched in the window of the colonel's house overlooking the town's main square, the sensuous *mulata* initiates the novel's second chapter with her "lament" of loneliness (*Gabriela*, 113). For, despite the opulent life-style with which the colonel rewards her services, she is considered his private property and is forbidden all contact with the outside world during his many prolonged absences from Ilhéus (*Gabriela*, 119–24). Thus, alone and gazing amorously through her window at the passing men below, Glória silently beckons them to enter and put an end to her imposed solitude:

> I am the colonel's Glória,
> The one with the fire in her breast,
> Who on her bedsheet
> Lies with loneliness.
> ....
> Push open my door,
> I have removed the bar
> And there is no key to lock it.
> Come extinguish my burning ember,
> Come burn yourself in my fire,
> And bring a little bit of love
> For I have much to give.
> Come share my bed.
>
> (*Gabriela*, 118)

Yet no man dares respond to her seductive overtures, for all are well aware of the colonel's reputation of sadistically punishing those who tamper with his concubines.

But one day Glória's loneliness is indeed terminated by Josué, the schoolmaster, who for some time has been preparing himself for the venture. Emboldened by an unsuccessful courtship of a planter's daughter, Malvina Tavares, he throws caution to the wind, disregarding the inevitable consequences in order to cross the *mulata*'s forbidden doorsill. Firmly convinced that a tragedy will occur once the jealous colonel learns of the liaison, the townspeople are again amazed by the unconventional outcome. Upon making the discovery, the deceived planter forsakes his violent reputation, merely evicting the couple from their expense-free rendezvous (*Gabriela,* 421–22).

Unlike the two previous heroines, Glória is cast in the role of a femme fatale. Scorned by the "virtuous" women of Ilhéus as a shameless harlot, to the men of the town she represents a forbidden fruit, a constant temptation in their midst. She is likewise viewed as a public utility, a social necessity by a segment of the male population (*Gabriela,* 182). For by her presence in their sexual fantasies she is said to enable married men to perform their husbandly duties in admirable fashion, however unattracted they may be by the physical attributes of their frigid, matronly wives (*Gabriela,* 155). In other words, she is not only the eternal temptress but also the means by which the men of Ilhéus are able to rationalize and perpetuate the myth of their wives' virginal purity and sexual indifference.

But Glória's uniqueness does not end here. Superimposed on her sirenic image is one of a helpless maiden desperately awaiting the arrival of a conquering hero to effect her rescue. Indeed, the author's ironic treatment of Josué's successful entrance—like his biblical namesake, Joshua, he is depicted as bringing down walls—is nothing less than a mock-epic burlesque of the quest myths of bygone literature. Yet beneath this cloak of levity there is a satirical message, for although it may be considered absurd by some to compare a "fallen woman" to an innocent damsel, the juxtaposition serves to dispel the notion that the plight of a concubine is somehow not to be taken seriously.

Despite the seeming success of her emancipation, Glória is in the final analysis no less dependent on the men in her life than are her affluent counterparts. In order to gain her freedom, she has had to rely on Josué, and once this is accomplished, she has no recourse but to attach herself to one man or another in order to avoid having to make her living as a common prostitute. For she is trained to do nothing else. Thus, when the impoverished schoolteacher offers to support her on his meager earnings, she turns him down. Instead, she agrees to a ménage à trois involving Josué and the liberal Col. Ribeirinho, for the

---

latter is far more able to maintain her in the style to which she is accustomed.

Malvina, the daughter of Col. Melk Tavares, is at once the youngest and most rebellious of the novel's heroines. A modern-day Ofenísia, she is depicted in the introductory poem to chapter 3 as a prisoner in her garden, an innocent schoolgirl bound by the "flowers" of her traditional female upbringing to a future of obedient self-sacrifice as a devoted wife and mother:

> I am a prisoner in my garden
> With flowers I am chained.
> Help! They're going to smother me.
> Help! They're going to kill me.
> Help! They're going to marry me
> In a house to bury me
> Cooking in the kitchen
> Tidying up the mess
> Playing the piano
> Go to mass, confess.
> Help! They're going to marry me
> In the bed impregnate me.
> ....
> My husband, lord and master
> Controlling my whole life.
> Deciding what clothes I wear
> And also which perfume.
> Controlling my every desire
> Controlling my sleep.
> Controlling my body
> Even my very soul.
> My only right to weep.
> His right, to kill.
>
> (*Gabriela*, 196)

Her feelings are not unlike those expressed earlier by Ofenísia, but having inherited her father's unyielding determination, she loudly proclaims her unwillingness to follow in the footsteps of her passive foremothers or in those of her own docile mother, blindly submitting to unquestioned male authority: "I am not going to submit to a marriage arranged by my family, nor am I going to bury myself in some planter's kitchen or be the servant of some doctor or lawyer in Ilhéus. I just want to live my own life" (*Gabriela*, 274).

This burning wish is reflected in the types of books she reads—tales of love and adventure, which the community regards as unsuitable for the consumption of nice girls (*Gabriela,* 224–25, 279). "A woman who sets herself up as a scholar is shameless and wants to lose her virtue" (*Gabriela,* 278), lectures her father. Her independent-mindedness may also be seen in her short romance with Josué, which she promptly breaks off when the latter displays his overpossessiveness (*Gabriela,* 279). And finally it leads her to want to escape Ilhéus and everyone in it, whatever the cost. Thus, when Rômulo Vieira, a young engineer from the progressive South, appears on the scene for a brief stay, it matters little that he is a married man, for he represents her ticket to freedom, her knight in shining armor. With him she will ride away from the wagging tongues and oppressive restrictions of Ilhéus to a life unfettered by petty conventions.

But Vieira proves to be more cowardly than chivalrous. Warned to leave town by the indignant Melk Tavares, who discovers the two conversing in public, the terrified Rômulo sneaks away without saying good-bye to Malvina. For her part, the young lady, after sustaining a harsh beating at the hands of her tyrannical father, sends word for the suitor to meet her on the beach so that the two may make love and elope together. But when he fails to show up, she vows never again to depend on a man for her deliverance, recognizing, as one critic so aptly puts it, "that her dependence on him had been another sign of the feminine frailty to which she had become conditioned" (*Gabriela,* 271–82).[15] Thus, a short time later, when Malvina is sent to boarding school in the Bahian capital, news is received of her lone escape. It is not until many months later that she is discovered to have gone to São Paulo, where she is said to be living on her own, working in an office by day and attending school by night (*Gabriela,* 371–72).

Neither the typical virginal ingénue with her storybook existence nor the traditional disobedient daughter punished for her sins, Malvina represents a new breed of woman, self-reliant and secure in the notion that she is destined for a brilliant future. She is triumphant in her rebellion, where others have failed. But in order to achieve this, she has had to leave Ilhéus behind. For even in its rapid transition toward greater modernity, the town is still not ready to accept the degree of feminism that Malvina's needs demand. Nevertheless, by taking the drastic measure of running away from home, she has awakened the town to a greater awareness of the growing female aspirations for increased freedom of choice.[16]

Finally, there is Gabriela, with her fragrance of clove and her color of cinnamon. She is the freest and most natural of the novel's women. She is also the most enigmatic. Driven coastward by the great droughts of the northeastern backlands, the humble young *mulata* arrives in Ilhéus barefoot and penniless, but is promptly hired by bar owner Nacib Saad to do his cooking chores. Her lovemaking talents prove to be the equal of her superb culinary skills; soon she and Nacib are lovers, sharing their bed and board. But the Arab merchant is not content to accept her as she is. In order to have her all to himself, he insists on making her Mrs. Saad. Here the trouble begins, for Nacib now tries to mold her into a "respectable" middle-class lady, subordinating her true nature to his image of the proper wife. In the process, Gabriela loses her identity as well as her cherished freedom.

Her symbolic imprisonment is treated by the introductory verses in mock-exotic style. Nacib is costumed as an Oriental sultan; Gabriela, as his captive queen:

> Oh, Sultan, what have you done
> To my happy girl?
>
> To a royal ball
> I took your happy girl
> Dressed in a regal gown.
> She talked with princesses,
> Chatted with scholars,
> Danced foreign dances,
> Drank the most expensive wines,
> Tasted fruit from Europe
> And was embraced by the King
> As a real, authentic Queen.
>
> Oh, Sultan, what have you done
> To my happy girl?
>
> Send her back to the kitchen,
> To her yard full of guavas,
> To her humble dances,
> To her calico dress,
> To her green slippers,
> To her innocent thoughts,
> To her uninhibited laughter,
> To her lost childhood,

> To her sighs in bed,
> To her passion for loving.
> Why do you wish to change her?
> (*Gabriela*, 276)

Why indeed? She had accepted his marriage proposal, not wanting to offend him. But he had forbidden her to enjoy all the pleasures of life, all the things that made her Gabriela.

It was awful being married. She didn't like it at all. The closet full of pretty dresses. More than three pairs of tight-fitting shoes. He even gave her jewelry. . . . What was she going to do with all those things? She was not allowed to do all the things she liked. . . . She couldn't walk barefoot on the sidewalk by the house. She couldn't run along the beach with the wind blowing her disheveled hair and her feet in the water. She couldn't laugh whenever she wanted to, wherever she was, in the presence of others. She couldn't say whatever came to mind. All that she liked she was not allowed to do. She was Mrs. Saad, so she couldn't. It was awful being married. (*Gabriela*, 366)

Just like the sad songbird that Nacib had given her, she was imprisoned inside a cage (*Gabriela*, 257ff.).

But Gabriela's "captivity" comes to an abrupt end when suddenly Nacib learns that all the while she has been sleeping with other men. Catching her in bed with a friend, he beats her and sends her away, but is unable to carry out the "unwritten law" (*Gabriela*, 391ff.). Ashamed of his "cowardice," Nacib considers leaving Ilhéus, but is persuaded to stay and to annul the marriage, whereupon he is hailed by the townsfolk as their most "civilized citizen." Months later, Nacib once again asks Gabriela to become his cook and she accepts. They renew their passionate relationship—but this time only as equals, without the subjugation of one to the other.

Gabriela defies easy classification. She seems to have something of several of the traditional female stereotypes, without wholly conforming to any one of them. Like Glória, she is a temptress, but more in a positive than in a negative sense. She attracts men not to exploit them, depend on them, or lead them astray, but simply because she enjoys being with them and sharing their love. Nor is her power of attraction purely physical. Shortly after her marriage to Nacib, Gabriela, unable to resist the excitement of a popular religious pageant, kicks off her shoes at a fashionable New Year's Eve ball and leads the cream of *ilheense* society in a plebeian dance (*Gabriela*, 377–85). Indeed, throughout the novel she seems to be something of a benevolent sorceress; she, along with Nacib, is credited with having exercised a strong influence on the outcome of situations as diverse as Glória's "liberation" and Col. Jesuíno Mendonça's murder conviction. Her charisma is referred to by one enlightened townsman as "that force that makes revolutions, that promotes discoveries" (*Gabriela*, 387).

She is likewise a motherly figure, strongly identified with the earth, simplicity, and tradition, given to generosity and self-sacrifice and protective of the helpless underdog, be it a caged songbird (*Gabriela*, 260–61), a stray tomcat (*Gabriela*, 230), or a hired killer on the run (*Gabriela*, 349–50). Yet she is a motherly figure who does not feel the social necessity of motherhood.

It is in her role as Nacib's companion, however, that Gabriela most departs from the traditional mold. She is anything but the virginal, pedestaled helpmate that Ilhéus is used to. She enjoys her sexuality both before and after marriage. She is never exploited, for as one critic points out, "she is a being who gives of herself freely and at almost all times seems to be in control of her emotional destinies."[17] As a lover she satisfies and is herself fulfilled; unlike the concubines she has her freedom. As a wife she is a failure, for in the Ilhéus of 1925 married women as much as concubines are still a type of chattel to be guarded. Even as an adulteress—the stereotype of the "bad wife"—she fails to meet with the traditional fate.

In a sense Gabriela is more symbolic than real. Her lack of sophistication at times renders her almost implausibly naive as a flesh-and-blood female character.[18] As is the case with the other heroines of the novel, her thoughts and emotions, simple though they may be, are amply explored through the author's use of the indirect free style. Yet she seems not to undergo any major psychological changes herself while, in the manner of a catalyst, she causes profound changes to occur in others and in the society around her.[19] It is not that she is a totally unidimensional character, simply that she is static, uncomplicated, and predictable, as one would expect of a caricature or stereotype. Her idealization as the quintessential *mulata* merely serves to strengthen the suspicion that she is intended to be something other than a "normal" realistic character. Indeed, the author himself hints at this symbolic role in the title of chapter 4: "The Moonlight of Gabriela [Perhaps a child, or the common people, who knows?]" (*Gabriela*, 303).[20] Yet, symbol or no, Gabriela is undeniably the motivating force of the novel.

There are other women in the book whom we might wish to discuss, given the opportunity: Mrs. Grant, the Englishwoman, who scandalizes the Ilhéus of 1925 with her habits of an emancipated female (*Gabriela*, 244–45); Jerusa, the granddaughter of the town's longtime political chieftain, with her admiration for Gabriela (*Gabriela*, 356ff., 384); the Dos Reis sisters, aging spinsters whose religious devotion is exceeded only by the sharpness of their tongues (*Gabriela*, 73–80, 120–21, 269–70); the flirtatious Iracema (*Gabriela*, 129, 246); the prudish Celestina (*Gabriela*, 129); and the nameless, shrinking mother of Malvina (*Gabriela*, 273–75). But all are relatively one-dimensional, unimportant figures compared to the five heroines examined above. And it is the latter who best illustrate the novelist's intentions.

By undermining and reversing some of the conventional female images found in literature, Amado seeks to illustrate through changing female role alternatives the movement toward greater freedom in a society evolving from a late feudalistic to an early capitalistic economy. This is not to say that he uses the women characters for purely symbolic reasons, rather that he regards their real-life counterparts as primary indicators of the transition to a new and freer economic, political, and social order.

It is true that to some extent this concern for women's emancipation on the novelist's part is motivated by a larger, neoromantic commitment to defending the rights of the poor and the underdog. Amado's populist views are well known and have been the subject of a number of articles.[21] Yet this in no way diminishes the sincerity of *Gabriela* as a feminist statement. If anything, it tends to confirm it.

Indeed, it would appear that Amado feels the liberation of women to be a necessary condition for any meaningful social progress to occur. The novel's women characters are not the only ones imprisoned in rigid sex roles; by perpetuating their confinement, the men of Ilhéus bind themselves to the role of defending that confinement at all costs. It is "expected" of Jesuíno Mendonça that he strictly enforce the "unwritten law" in order to reassert his manhood. Nacib, too, feels compelled by the social pressures of his community to observe the barbarous custom in order to "cleanse his honor."

To regard *Gabriela* as a feminist statement, then, is not to claim that it depicts the total liberation of Brazilian women. Nor is it to assert that Amado, a male, is entirely free of the sexist biases of his gender and generation. The end of the "unwritten law" and the gradual lessening of the seclusion of *ilheense* women must be viewed in their proper context as early, though significant, steps in the movement toward female equality. Only then can we begin to appreciate the novel, for all its restrictions, as an important precursor of the later feminist works of modern Brazilian and Latin American literature.

Chapter Four

Two Exercises in Structured Ambiguity

Of Dual Identities and Multiple Truths

The greater degree of ironic detachment with which Amado has approached action and characters in much of his latter-day fiction has been most pronounced in the works that emphasize the relativity of truth. Nowhere is this more important than in the two novelettes originally published as *Os velhos marinheiros*. Both *A morte e a morte de Quincas Berro D'água* and *A completa verdade sobre as discutidas aventuras do Comandante Vasco Moscoso de Aragão, capitão de longo curso* deliberately leave the reader with considerable doubt as to the reality or irreality of the events they narrate. This they achieve primarily through the use of such ironic devices as multiple and unreliable narrators, contrapuntal internal reduplications, and double perspective. Of these, the last-named has perhaps received the least attention.

Amado first employs double perspective in *Quincas*. In addition to highlighting the subjectivity of conflicting versions of the truth, it comically underscores existing differences in class values and priorities. The petit bourgeois family of the late, lamented Joaquim Soares da Cunha, alias Quincas Berro D'água, considers his autumnal sowing of wild oats to be an embarrassment, his life having ended for them the day of his abrupt departure from polite society several years earlier. When confronted with the fait accompli of his actual death, they are only too happy to lay him to rest with as little fanfare and expense as possible and without any further humiliation for themselves. To his skid-row companions—and to Quincas himself—however, his life began only when at the age of fifty he abandoned wife and family, thus repudiating the drab existence of Joaquim Soares da Cunha. His belated devotion to a liberated lifestyle has elevated him in their eyes to the status of a folk hero, and with his passing their lives have been impoverished.

Joaquim-Quincas is thus endowed with a dual identity, one for each social class. Indeed, much of the ironic humor and social satire of the work stems from the direct confrontation of these two diametrically opposite points of view—the one more materialistic, the other more spiritual. While the early and final chapters deal separately with the reactions of both parties, one of the later episodes, the wake scene, juxtaposes the two "families" and their conflicting social values, as if to represent a symbolic enactment of the class struggle. Decked out in the garb of a bourgeois, Quincas is barely recognizable to his humble associates (*Quincas*, 48). To Vanda, his daughter, Joaquim in death had seemed finally to submit to her iron will and, by extension, to that of her dead mother, whom he had abandoned. She had at last succeeded in erasing his defiant smile; no longer did she "imagine" hearing his earthy expletives arising from the open coffin. But with the arrival of the four "vagrants," he seems to have regained his stubborn rebelliousness, the contemptuous smirk on his lifeless face having strangely reappeared (*Quincas*, 49).

The full force of Amado's biangular portrayal of Joaquim-Quincas is not felt, however, until after the withdrawal of the Cunha family from the wake. The focus now shifts away from the conflicting social ethics implicit in the dual identity to the very question of whether Joaquim-Quincas is actually dead, as had been presumed, or merely "playing possum" to humiliate his snobbish relatives. The reality of his every "action" and "reaction" is thus rendered ambiguous by the novelist. This is accomplished in part by the narrator's repeated use of such expressions as *parecia* ([it] seemed), *pelo jeito* (by the looks of it), and *evidentemente* (evidently) to qualify the description of the hero's apparent attitudes and feelings.

The several utterances ascribed to Berro D'água toward the end of the wake, though if true plainly indicate that he is still alive, may also be interpreted as hallucinations induced by the convenient drunkenness of the four remaining mourners. Yet it is never completely clear which of these interpretations the reader is supposed to accept. An additional quantum of ambiguity is generated by the narrator's use of double entendres and his description of Quincas's movements with verbs that connote voluntary action. Thus during the drunken romp toward the waterfront to which the four companions drag the would-be corpse, Quincas is equivocally described as being "satisfeito da vida" (exceedingly happy) (*Quincas*, 59), "num dos seus melhores dias" (in one of his better days) (*Quincas*, 60), and "no melhor de sua forma" (in the best of shape) (*Quincas*, 63). It is further noted that "Quincas was almost running, stumbling on the stones" (*Quincas*, 62), that at one point he tried to trip his comrades while sticking his tongue out at passersby (*Quincas*, 60), and that finally "Quincas rose to his feet" (*Quincas*, 65) before "diving" into the sea. Thus the ambiguity is gleefully maintained.

Perhaps the major bone of contention to separate the dichotomous views of Joaquim-Quincas is the manner, time, and place of his extinction. Although the narrator sets out to unravel the mystery, in the end the decision as to where the truth lies is left up to the reader. If, as the Cunha family contends, the demented patriarch expired quietly in a filthy cubicle on the Ladeira do Tabuão, then logically the account of those who claim to have seen Quincas plunge voluntarily into the surf of All Saints' Bay is a canard concocted by a band of drunken miscreants. If, on the other hand, Quincas was still alive throughout the wake and subsequently joined his comrades for a final fling before taking his own life in the waves, then it is safe to surmise that the entire death scenario was an elaborate hoax on his haughty kin. The only other alternative—death and resurrection—is at once the least logically possible and the most symbolically satisfying. For if we admit the possibility of Quincas's magically transcending death to preserve his cherished freedom, then we have already gone a long way toward invalidating the kinds of hypocrisy and petty materialism that so provoked his angry rebellion. Yet again we are never told which one of these realities to accept; the narrative remains open-ended.

In any event, both the hero's twofold identity and the amusing controversy surrounding his death serve primarily to set forth in a nonthreatening, seemingly disinterested fashion the fundamental economic divergences that underlie the two contradictory *ethoi* in question. Thus by employing a double perspective the author succeeds in effectively conveying his ideological message while also managing to entertain his readership.

A second and equally artistic form of double perspective emerges in *Comandante*. Vasco is seen by his retinue of admirers as a swashbuckling hero of the seven seas; he is drawn by his detractors as a grocery heir and flagrant hoaxer. Vested interests motivate the positions of both parties. The former seek to preserve in Vasco what they feel to be their own just parcel of greatness, while the latter endeavor to aggrandize themselves by exposing the "master mariner" as a phony.

Vasco, however, is not the only one in the story to receive a binary characterization. Depending on which version of the comandante's life is believed, Johann is either a Swedish sailor (*Comandante,* 97) or a Swedish tobacco exporter (*Comandante,* 158); Soraia, an exotic Arab dancer or a Brazilian dance-hall entertainer (*Comandante,* 158); Menendez, an ill-tempered shipowner or a heartless food wholesaler (*Comandante,* 148); Giovanni, an Italian seaman or an elderly black stockroom employee (*Comandante,* 151); and Robert or Roberto, a rich, abdominous Britisher or a wealthy Bahian playboy (*Comandante,* 143).

Two characters, Carol and Dorothy, are supplied with at least three personalities apiece. By one of Vasco's accounts, Carol is an opium smuggler in the East Indian seaport of Makassar (*Comandante,* 106), while in another she is represented as Sister Carol, a devout Asian missionary (*Comandante,* 290). Yet according to Chico Pacheco she is in reality the proprietress of a noted Salvador brothel (*Comandante,* 141). Again, if one can believe the captain's tales, Dorothy, a passenger on one of the many ships under his command, succumbed to yellow fever after renouncing both husband and fortune to spend her life with the seafaring hero (*Comandante,* 105–7, 289–90). If, on the other hand, Chico is telling the truth, Dorothy is a kept woman kidnapped by Vasco's friends in Bahia so that she and Vasco may be able to carry on a passionate love affair (*Comandante,* 143, 174–80). Still a third alternative, appearing in one of Vasco's alleged dreams of grandeur, pictures Dorothy as the alluring spouse of the Bahian secretary of transportation, who has come to dedicate a rail line constructed by the renowned "Doutor Vasco Moscoso de Aragão, civil engineer" (*Comandante,* 166).

In *Quincas* the decedent's two identities are presented not as mutually exclusive realities but as successive periods in his life. The only real dispute over the "objective" truth, then, centers on the circumstances of his untimely death. Barring some sort of miraculous resurrection, the reader must choose one account or the other, or else provide a plausible compromise. With Vasco, however, each version of his past existence seems to preclude the other. He is either a seasoned mariner or a posturing landlubber, but not both.

Or so it seems, at least, until he is called upon to take command of a captainless ship bound for Recife and points north. Oddly enough, throughout this "initiation ordeal" the two realities appear juxtaposed in Vasco's thoughts and statements, as though they formed a harmonious continuum. He is at once the Aragãozinho of grocery fame and the intrepid conqueror of the briny deep, a frequenter of Salvador's Pensão Monte Carlo and a habitué of oriental cabarets, an acquaintance

of the Bahian governor and an on-the-scene defender of the Portuguese
crown (*Comandante,* 231, 236, 247, 250, 252, 283, 292). Not satis-
fied with only two antithetical options with which to mislead his reading audience, the novelist thus has further clouded the picture by
mischievously hinting at a third, hybrid thesis, which seems to raise
as many questions as it purports to solve.

It might be argued that one convenient way to represent the resulting structure of *Comandante* would be in the tripartite schema of thesis,
antithesis, and synthesis.[1] Yet this is true only to a limited degree, for
although there occurs in the end an interpenetration of thesis and antithesis, the very fact that this is done primarily to confuse the reader
further means that the synthesis must remain only partially actualized.
Only the least controversial elements of the conflicting first and second
perspectives are homogenized to form the third. There is never any
attempt to explain away the sharpest points of disagreement, for they
cannot be explained away. Like *Quincas, Comandante* is in the final analysis essentially open-ended. And this open-endedness results not so
much from the creation of multiple, overlapping truths as it does from
the interplay of two diametrically opposite points of view.

On the one hand, Amado seems to be calling attention to the futility
of trying to recover the truth from either of the two conflicting perspectives, for both contain serious internal inconsistencies. On the
other hand, he appears to be suggesting that even the reconciliation of
the two into a cohesive synthesis may be difficult—at least, if we expect to eliminate all points of disagreement. As in the Hegelian dialectic, any such synthesis will itself necessarily become another thesis
with its own innate contradictions and need for resolution in another
synthesis. What is more, no two syntheses will be identical. Faced
with the open-endedness of the two tales, every reader will attempt to
reconcile the incongruities in a third perspective. But in the end even
this perspective will prove to be partial to the extent that it is influenced by the reader's personal biases and circumstances. Thus every
reader in effect will create a unique version of the truth.

The sociological implications are not difficult to draw. By associating the conflicting perspectives in the two works with opposing social
classes or community ethics, Amado seeks to show that no single class
or ethic is capable of unilaterally satisfying human needs. Difficult
though it may be to attain, only a synthesis of some sort can provide
a workable solution for society's problems. And no two solutions will

be the same. Each will inevitably be influenced by the preexisting tendencies and partialities of the society in question.

Amado's ultimate solutions for the two tales do little to resolve the factual contradictions raised by the double perspectives. Quincas's hinted resurrection and Vasco's heaven-sent storm (a deus ex machina) are in the final analysis nothing more than wish fulfillments used to implement the author's notions of poetic justice. The question of what is real and what is unreal is left for the reader to determine.

Thus the use of double perspective, while allowing Amado greater latitude to treat his characters ironically, does not prevent him from displaying his partisanship. He reserves the right to create and take sides in parallel double perspectives and to resolve ambiguities by imposing his own authorial will. Having explored the diverse facets of truth, he acknowledges its relativity, but shows this relativity to be socially conditioned. Double perspective thus serves him as a means of translating the various moral and social cleavages into discrepancies of opinion and perception. Yet because of its seeming dispassion it also affords him the luxury of weaving his own whimsical truth while still preserving a thin veil of impartiality.

The Gospel according to Saint Jorge?

In a 1969 article, "The 'New' Jorge Amado," Elizabeth Schlomann Lowe mentions having detected in the story of Quincas Berro D'água "a bizarre parallel" with the death and resurrection of Christ.[2] Affonso Romano de Sant'Anna briefly explores that interpretation in an essay published in 1983, but does not elaborate greatly on its implications.[3] The case for a biblical parody in *Quincas* would indeed seem to be a strong one. There is nothing in the novelette to warrant the presumption of an allegory. Nor is it likely that the novelist intended to write a full-blown "Evangelho segundo Jorge Amado." Yet such elements as the protagonist's resurrection and appearance before disciples (*Quincas,* 48–59), his rejection of water for *cachaça* (white rum) (*Quincas,* 40), the last *peixada* (fish fry) (*Quincas,* 64), and the division of his garments (*Quincas,* 56) do tend to remind us, however vaguely, of similar events in Jesus' life, death, and rebirth. And those elements seem to be not coincidental but rather part of a deliberate, albeit jumbled, pastiche of the events recounted in the Gospels, particularly the Passion.

Quincas is the story of a middle-aged minor public official who abandons family and middle-class respectability to spend his remaining years in the company of Bahia's rogues and prostitutes. The story opens with the news of his death in a filthy cubicle on the Ladeira do Tabuão. There are flashbacks recounting his life as a vagrant. But the bulk of the narrative is a comparison of the reactions and manifestations of grief shown by Quincas's two "families": his flesh and blood relatives, on the one hand, and his band of ne'er-do-well followers, on the other. We witness the former's hastily convened family council in a cheap restaurant on the Baixa dos Sapateiros. Both there and on an earlier occasion in the family home at Itapagipe the conversation centers around just how to lay the remains to rest without incurring further embarrassment to the family. Most of the rituals of mourning of the humble classes are set in the streets, on the docks, and in the brothels of Salvador. Amado characterizes their grief as being far more sincere than that of Quincas's materialistic kin.

The climax of the narrative begins with the wake scene. Both "families" are assembled in Quincas's cubicle for the simple rite. Driven by practical concerns and a feeling of contempt for Quincas's ragged friends, the real family makes an early departure, leaving the corpse alone with the latter. Whether by magic or as a result of the drunkenness of the four remaining mourners, once his relatives have left Quincas appears to come alive, joking with his companions and downing his share of the rum. Whereupon it is remembered that there was to be a fish fry at the docks on that night. Thus, the four friends remove Quincas from the coffin and drag him down to the waterfront for a seafood dinner. During the merrymaking, which occurs on the boat of a friend outside the breakwater, a storm arises. In the confusion, Quincas is seen to stand up and heard to utter several words of wisdom before diving into the stormy waves of the bay.

Three types of symbolism dominate the pastiche. The first, reversed symbolism, carries patently irreverent overtones; it contributes to the work's macabre, or black, humor. The second involves geographical and cultural displacement: characters, objects, and events are stylized in terms of present-day Bahia. And the third, condensation, is responsible for the jumbled nature. Many events and characters in *Quincas* are *overdetermined,* to use Freud's term. That is to say, instead of corresponding to single scriptural events and characters, they are plurally motivated, deliberately recalling two or more elements of the parodied biblical text.[4]

The first technique may be seen, for example, in the gesture of mourning accorded the fallen hero by the harlots of Bahia: "several of the women decided not to be with men on that night. They were in mourning, as if it were Holy Thursday or Good Friday" (*Quincas*, 41). The substitution of the *peixada* for the Last Supper (Matt. 26:26–29; Mark 14:22–25; Luke 22:19) and the replacement of the water/vinegar deception (John 19:28–30) with one involving *cachaça* and water exemplify the second technique. The third technique is evident in the march through Pelourinho (discussed in paragraph 12 below). There are many instances of all three procedures and frequent overlapping.

Following is a list of additional parallels that might be included in the case for a pastiche:

1.   Quincas's early life, like Christ's, is that of a normal man, his new life having begun at the age of fifty (Christ's earthly ministry began at thirty).

2.   Although both Jesus and Quincas are heroes among the people, rebels against hypocrisy and false idols, and friends to thieves, prostitutes, and humble Samaritans, Quincas is no paragon of continence and holiness. Nevertheless, his profligate behavior and that of his friends are held up as a positive standard against the pharisaical, materialistic, and often petty code of conduct sponsored by the lower middle class.

3.   While Jesus is often referred to in the New Testament and elsewhere with epithets of a positive nature, such as "Son of God," "Son of Man," "Prince of Peace," "King of Kings," "Lamb of God," "Light of the World," "Lord," and "Messiah," Quincas has been given such dubious designations as "king of the vagabonds of Bahia" (*Quincas*, 33), "king of the honky-tonks" (*Quincas*, 34), "patriarch of the red-light district" (*Quincas*, 34), "grand drunkard of Salvador" (*Quincas*, 33), "ragged philosopher of the marketplace" (*Quincas*, 33), "senator of the honky-tonks" (*Quincas*, 33), "vagrant par excellence" (*Quincas*, 33), "our father" (*Quincas*, 44), "the good man" (*Quincas*, 44), and "the light of the night" (*Quincas*, 45). When one of Quincas's four close friends informs another of the death of "our father," a smart aleck in the crowd asks for a clarification: "Jesus Christ or the Governor?" (*Quincas*, 46).

4.   Neither Christ (Mark 6:4) nor Quincas is a prophet in his own land: "An old sailor without a ship or an ocean, demoralized on dry land, but through no fault of his own" (*Quincas*, 38–39). Furthermore, neither considers the earth, or dry land, his home: "I am not of this world," (John 8:23);[5] "He would rise to his feet, his body swaying, the cachaça giving him that staggering equilibrium common to men of the sea, and declare his status as an 'old salt,'" (*Quincas*, 38); "It was in his blood. He didn't need to learn any-

thing about sailing; he had been born knowing how," (*Quincas*, 39).

5.   Ironically, Quincas is referred to by his relatives as a "cross" to bear, who had turned their lives into a "Calvary," even though the designations might better have been used by him to describe his life with them before his autumnal liberation.

6.   Again ironically, Quincas is said to be the son of Madalena, an indirect reference to Mary Magdalene (Luke 7:37–50), who, along with the Virgin Mary, mother of Jesus, is one of the six women known by that first name in the New Testament.

7.   While Jesus is baptized by John the Baptist in the Jordan River (Matt. 3:13–17; Mark 1:9–11; Luke 3:21–22), Quincas is dubbed with the epithet "Berro D'água" (Water Yell) as the result of the *cachaça*-water deception in a local bar (*Quincas*, 40). The latter incident also brings to mind the water-vinegar episode of the crucified Messiah (John 19:28–30), as mentioned above.

8.   In Matthew 23:33 Jesus brands the Pharisees as "serpents," as a "brood of vipers." Curiously, Quincas employs the same uncommon epithet—"Vipers!" (*Quincas*, 35)—to address his wife and daughter just before he abandons them and their pharisaical ways.

9.   The *negra*'s finding Quincas's body lying on the dirty bedsheets of his cot (*Quincas*, 20–21) is vaguely reminiscent of Mary Magdalene's finding Jesus's tomb empty (Matt. 28:1; Mark 16:1–4; Luke 24:1–3; John 20:1,2). In the first case, the *negra* had come to Quincas to get some herbs for a religious celebration and had found the door open. In the second case, Mary Magdalene had come to the tomb with spices to embalm Christ's body, which had been wrapped in a linen shroud. She had found the boulder rolled away from the opening and the body gone.

10.   Jesus is resurrected from the dead and appears subsequently before his disciples (Mark 16:14; Luke 24:36–49; John 20:19–23). Quincas, too, comes back to life after dying and appears before his four closest companions (*Quincas*, 56ff.).

11.   Jesus' garments are divided by the soldiers after he is crucified, and lots are cast for them (John 19:23–25). Quincas's burial clothes are divided up among his four companions, who need them more than he does (*Quincas*, 56).[6]

12.   Quincas's triumphant march through Pelourinho on his way to the waterfront (*Quincas,* 60ff.) recalls both the entry of Christ into Jerusalem before the Crucifixion (Matt. 21:1–11; Mark 11:1–11; Luke 19:29–44; John 12:12–19) and the road to Calvary (Matt. 27:31–34; Mark 15:20–23; Luke 23:26–32; John 19:16,17).

13.   Jesus angrily expels vendors and money changers from the temple in Jerusalem, whipping them and overturning their tables (John 2:13–22). Quincas and friends oust a group of marijuana smokers from a local bar after a free-for-all that overturns tables, breaks a large number of glasses and bottles, and leaves several persons sprawled out on the barroom floor (*Quincas,* 63).

14.   While Jesus walks on water from shore to boat (Matt. 14:25–33; John 6:16–21), Quincas dives from a boat into the water (*Quincas,* 66). Quincas's final plunge before a boatful of witnesses is also reminiscent of Christ's Ascension into heaven (Mark 16:19–20; Luke 24:50–53). Quincas's descent, like Christ's ascent, is made with pronouncements of prophetic wisdom, but with no promise to return to earth. Here the symbolism of water and depth replaces that of space and height. The return to the security of the maternal womb is portrayed not by a celestial paradise but by the freedom and expanse of the sea.

15.   Cataclysmic phenomena accompany the death of Jesus on the Cross (Matt. 27:45, 51–52; Mark 5:33, 38; Luke 23:44–45). Quincas's descent into the waves is marked by five bolts of lightning and deafening thunder (*Quincas,* 65–66).

16.   Quincas's relatives find an empty coffin (*Quincas,* 67), calling to mind the empty tomb of the resurrected Christ.

17.   Several Christian symbols are prominent in *Quincas.* Of these, the two most important are the fish and the frog. The former, associated since the early Christian era with the figure of Christ, is present more by implication than in fact.[7] Water symbolism, the sea, old sailors, waterfront pronouncements, boats, fishermen, and fish frys pervade the narrative. Quincas chooses the sea as the site of his own burial, perhaps in the belief that he is returning to Janaína, or Iemanjá, the Afro-Bahian goddess of the waters, who is said to beckon sailors and fishermen to her side. More important to the story, though, is the frog, for it seems to have been the bullfrog placed in the coffin by one of Quincas's friends that acted as a catalyst in bringing about the supposed resurrection. According to J. E. Cirlot in his *Dictionary of Symbols,* the frog has had a long symbolic association with both creation and resurrection, having been incorporated by the early Christians into their symbolism.[8]

These are some of the most obvious parallels that can be drawn between the story of Quincas Berro D'água and the Passion. Doubtless, there are others, but these are probably sufficient to lead even the most skeptical of readers to a serious consideration of the thesis. Admittedly, the disjointed character of the pastiche, the use of reversed symbolism, and the frequent lack of clear-cut correspondences do tend to obscure the author's intentions. Yet it should not be difficult to describe the process he uses to incorporate elements of the Passion into his tale.

Amado apparently starts by fragmenting the Passion into its various fundamental components (characters, sequences, symbols, and so on). He then reconstitutes the story by reassembling these components to suit his own purposes, creating another whole and thus giving new meaning to both components and totality. His reasons for doing this, however, are not altogether clear.

If we accept the idea that Amado has sought to rewrite the Passion according to his own beliefs, what are the various implications? Are we to believe that he has created this pastiche in order to cast a veil of skepticism on the official version of the Passion? Perhaps he is attempting to call into question such an event as the disappearance of Christ's body after the Crucifixion (cf. Matt. 28:13). Or maybe he has incorporated elements of the Passion into *Quincas* not in order to make a statement about biblical events but rather to show the applicability of an ancient message to the modern world. What better way to attack the confinement and hypocrisy of present-day Christian society than to relate the current situation to that which, according to Christian belief, was so roundly condemned by God himself?

The possibilities are numerous. Yet whatever the author's intentions in composing the pastiche, there is no doubt about the message that *Quincas* imparts. It is a celebration of the freedom of the individual and a criticism of the rules of polite society insofar as they needlessly restrict that freedom. It is also an "epic of free will," as some have called it, for by transcending death itself to reassert his will Quincas assumes epic stature alongside the larger-than-life heroes of bygone times. It is difficult in this day to recall a more blindly optimistic precept than the final words of Berro D'água: "Everyone take care of his own funeral. Nothing is impossible" (*Quincas,* 15).

Chapter Five
Dona Flor e seus dois maridos: A Blending of Disparate Realities

Sociopolitical symbolism

Dona Flor is, after *Gabriela, cravo e canela,* probably the best known of Amado's novels, some of its popularity having come from the success of the film version.[1] It tells the story of one Florípedes Paiva, a young, lower middle-class cooking teacher in Salvador, Bahia, whose marriage to a promiscuous, ne'er-do-well gambler, Vadinho Guimarães, is suddenly terminated by his premature death. Despite his disgraceful habits and constant exploitation of her, Flor is devastated, for the rogue was also her greatest source of pleasure and spiritual fulfillment with his zest for life and his taste for fine foods and uninhibited lovemaking. Though modest and shy by nature, she had defied both family and friends to marry him and, with his death, she feels that her life has ended.

Within a short time, however, Flor finds herself emotionally and sexually vulnerable. Determined never to remarry, she tries to repress her sexual desires, which she considers unbecoming in a loyal, grieving widow. "Only a shameless woman, without love for her husband, could still think of such disgusting things—how disgraceful!" she reasons with traditional self-abasement (*Dona Flor,* 186). Yet her erotic fantasies persist. The more she tries to dispel them, the stronger her neurosis becomes. She begins to perceive "disgusting" sexual interpretations in everything that she sees and reads. In her sleep, she is tormented by ever more vivid erotic dreams. Thus, although outwardly she appears to be content with her life of celibacy—to be the "perfect widow," so to speak—inwardly she is full of pent-up sexual frustrations and on one occasion almost succumbs to the romantic advances of a notorious neighborhood Lothario.

Flor is thus only too happy to put an end to her hunger for male

companionship a short time later by accepting the marriage proposal
of Dr. Teodoro Madureira, a prosperous and respectable, if somewhat
stuffy, local pharmacist. But security and respectability prove to be
insufficient to her needs. She longs for the rapture and excitement that
only Vadinho was able to supply. In response to this, the latter reap-
pears as a ghost and is soon able to overcome her defenses and regain
his place in the marriage bed. Shortly thereafter, however, he begins
to disappear as the result of an Afro-Bahian *candomblé* ritual that she
had earlier ordered in an effort to thwart his "adulterous" overtures. It
is only through Flor's personal intercession that the decision of the
Yoruba gods—the *orixás*—is in the end reversed, thus assuring her
continued enjoyment of the best of both worlds.

This fanciful tale relies in large part for its mode of characterization—if not also its very structure—on a series of oppositions that
delineate the personalities of the two husbands. In a word, Teodoro is
everything that Vadinho is not, and vice versa. The two are seen to
contrast on everything from their eating and sexual habits (selectivity/
omnivorousness; monogamy/promiscuity) to their social status (bour-
geois/bohemian), musical tastes (highbrow/lowbrow), and their attitudes toward the work ethic (positive/negative). Teodoro is represented
as narrow-minded, straitlaced, unemotional, regimented, pious, and
highly respectable, while Vadinho is styled as tolerant, uninhibited,
passionate, spontaneous, irreverent, and utterly shameless. If one is
best characterized as the quintessential Homo sapiens, or perhaps
Homo faber, the other may be described quite aptly as a specimen of
Homo ludens.

It is in their relationship to Flor that the two spouses display their
greatest dissimilarities. Each may be seen to satisfy a different, albeit
important, part of her psychological needs. Though he is employed in
the municipal bureaucracy as a garden inspector, Vadinho spends most
of his time and money carousing and gambling. It is thus up to Flor
to pay for the couple's food and rent. Yet this is not always an easy
task, given Vadinho's penchant for extorting funds to support his vices
and help his friends. He is not above stealing from Flor, and on at least
one occasion he resorts to wife beating in order to obtain his gambling
money. He is also unfaithful to her time and again. But when he is
with her he is passionate in his lovemaking and unrestrained in his
attentions toward her. Thus their relationship is one of both love and
hate. Vadinho is to Flor both the cause of her greatest suffering and
the origin of her utmost joy.

Teodoro's treatment of Flor is quite different. He is faithful to her and is a good provider, a model of rectitude and Christian morality. For him a wife is something sacred, the mother of one's children, who should be treated with respect, restraint, and dignity. If Vadinho is free in his sexual behavior, Teodoro is prudish and insipid. He is a man without passions, whose only obsession is with method and moderation. So moderate and methodical are his habits that he actually sets up a schedule for the couple's sexual encounters: "on Wednesdays and Saturdays, at 10:00 P.M., give or take a minute . . . with an encore on Saturdays and the possibility of one on Wednesdays" (*Dona Flor*, 325). With him, Flor's life becomes a monotonous routine of visits, lectures, meetings, and musical recitals, devoid of the color and excitement she had previously known. It is this utter mediocrity that proves to be his downfall and leads in the end to Vadinho's return.

On a personal level, then, Dona Flor's story is one that is based on the formula of thesis, antithesis, and synthesis. She moves from a position of dependence on one rather unidimensional man to one of dependence on another, in every way his opposite. Both prove to be unfulfilling, and only by combining the best aspects of both is she ultimately able to take control of her life and begin to live it on her own terms. Thus the Hegelian dialectic serves as the work's primary structuring principle. Instead of the traditional narrative in which either protagonist or antagonist emerges in the end as the clear-cut victor, we are confronted here with the need for a hybrid solution, one that will reconcile the best of the two competing forces while rejecting the worst.

It is here that the novel's sociopolitical symbolism begins to emerge. Some have seen in Vadinho a veiled characterization of Getúlio Vargas, whose dictatorial government ruled Brazil in the 1930s and early 1940s. Others have felt the work to be an allegory of the clash between the leftist populism of the 1950s and early 1960s and the positivist military and technocratic currents that came to oppose it. The very chronology of the novel's publication has always raised certain suspicions as to what may have been Amado's underlying purpose in writing it. It seems strange that a traditionally engagé leftist author, so recently divorced from prescriptive Marxist esthetics, should write and publish such an apparently frivolous work of fiction just two years after the imposition of a brutal military dictatorship. But *Dona Flor*'s superficial frivolity may belie the author's serious, underlying intent. Vadinho and Teodoro, with their conflicting class *ethoi,* are surely meant to represent something more than they at first appear to be. Even Flor, though more complicated psychologically, invites symbolic interpretation, with her need for more than what either husband can alone supply and her apparent ability to effect a magical synthesis of the two in order to satisfy it.

But what of the specifics of this interpretation? To accept the idea that *Dona Flor* is some sort of political allegory of the 1964 military takeover, we would probably have to equate Vadinho with the traditional liberal populist politicians (if not with President João Goulart himself), Teodoro with Marshal Humberto Castelo Branco and his clique of hard-line generals and technocrats, and Flor with Brazil, the Brazilian government or the Brazilian people. In such a case, however, we would also have to account for other characters and events within the same consistent allegorical scheme. While this might be possible in a few instances, it would appear to be especially difficult with such things as the two-year delay between Vadinho's death and Flor's second marriage and the final compromise solution achieved through the use of the supernatural.

The Vargas thesis presents similar obstacles. True, the love-hate relationship enjoyed by Flor and Vadinho might be likened to that of the Brazilian people with the late dictator, provided we ignore the apparent discrepancy between the novelist's largely sympathetic treatment of Vadinho and his oft-repeated contempt for Vargas. Vadinho's demise and subsequent return might also add credence to such an interpretation. But the allegorical view again begins to break down when we attempt to integrate such elements as the narrative's chronology, its denouement, and the other major characters into the scheme.

The problem with both of these explanations rests with their assumption of an allegory based on specific historical persons and events. It is fruitless to search for the type of strict one-to-one correspondences and chronological parallelisms that such a model would require, given the great number of apparent inconsistencies that exist. I should like to propose an alternative reading that, I think, is probably closer to what Amado had in mind. It is a blend of both allegory and fantasy that seems to account for all of the major elements of the story without incurring the problems of the preceding interpretations.

I would agree that, on one level, Vadinho is indeed meant to symbolize the traditional politics of populism in Brazil, and that Flor serves to represent the country and its people. Such things as Vadinho's government sinecure, his reputation for doing many favors, and his talents for sweet talk and extortion are reminiscent of the nepotism, demagoguery, and graft often associated with the Brazilian political parties of the 1930s, 1940s, 1950s, and early 1960s. Despite Vadinho's many shortcomings, Flor is hopelessly captivated by his passion, charm, and eloquent promises. She cannot do without him, but she needs much more than he alone can provide.

By the same token, Teodoro epitomizes the technocratic and military sectors of Brazilian society, both historically and at the time of the book's writing. If Vadinho is warm and emotional with Flor, the pharmacist's approach is one of cold rationalism, based on his love of order and restraint. He attempts to regiment her life not out of perversity but because he believes that happiness and material progress can come only through discipline. But in the end he too proves unequipped to deal with her spiritual needs. Her life becomes an endless routine of drab, uneventful occurrences, and she again comes to perceive that something is lacking.

Once more the political implications for Brazil seem clear. Order and discipline can lead to material progress for a nation, just as a warm, personalist approach to government can turn out to be spiritually fulfilling. Both have their negative aspects as well as their positive, and neither can be totally satisfying without the countervailing force of the other. If Brazil has had its share in recent decades of populist demagoguery and corrupt politicians, it has also had a history long before the latest dictatorships of those who thought they could save the country with simplistic military and developmental solutions. Few governments have been able to combine the positive aspects of both approaches while avoiding the negative.

A second level of symbolism, more social than political, may also be detected. Here the two husbands may be seen to represent the vices and virtues of their respective social classes. Again, Flor is meant to stand for Brazil, as the two competing class *ethoi,* embodied by the two spouses, vie with one another for her exclusive attentions. But once more each by itself is found to be unilateral and incomplete; the need for a synthesis is again apparent.

It is here that quasi-allegory turns into fantasy. On a symbolic level, the novel's magical resolution is not meant to reflect historical fact, but is rather a speculatory statement on Amado's part about what he sees as the inevitable solution to Brazil's continuing ordeal. Apparently, no one narrow sociopolitical philosophy is, in his opinion, capable of meeting the country's every need, whether it be populist and democratic in nature or technocratic and military, whether it is oriented to the values and requirements of the working classes or to those of the bourgeoisie. Only through a strong coalition of both of these forces can an effective and wholly satisfactory system be achieved. Brazil, like Flor, is otherwise incomplete.

Recipes, Menus, and Sensual Delights

Much of the satirical humor of *Dona Flor* involves the novelist's skillful blending of spicy Afro-Bahian folk recipes and menus into the surface structure of the narrative. Such interpolations are meant to recall, accentuate, and complement the work's immoderate measures of sex and sensuality. Ultimately, they also seek to invalidate middle-class inhibitions and to enhance the reader's gusto for the free, hedonistic lifestyle that the author associates with the Bahian poor.

Like the introductory poems of *Gabriela,* the recipes and menus of *Dona Flor* help to set the stage for each of the novel's major divisions. Both funnier and better integrated than their counterparts in the earlier novel, they are lyrically stylized renditions of actual culinary formulas, as Amado indicates on the book's cover flaps. In general their tone is rich with colloquialisms and small talk, thus preambling the gossipy narration of the incidents to follow. Because they are recurrent elements, recipes and menus also perform a unifying function, agglutinating the novel's disparate episodes.

Yet it is the sexual association of these interpolations that most contributes to the intensification of their satirical message. Eating and sex are likened to one another;[2] they are almost synonymous in the mind of the protagonist. Each of the two activities creates its own level of coherence through the course of the novel, across which are projected the personal and class differences of the main characters, particularly the two husbands. Expressed in terms of binary oppositions, the contrasts in dietary and sexual preferences of Vadinho and Teodoro are comically reinforced by the constant interplay of the two semantic levels. And since the acts of eating and lovemaking are among the human activities least expected to serve as class indicators, the wedding of the two planes of oppositions is rendered all the more effective as a means of spoofing the respective social classes.

The first recipe of the novel is contained in a memo reportedly sent to the novelist by the story's cooking-teacher heroine (*Dona Flor,* 15). It lists the ingredients and instructions for making *bolo de puba,* or *carimã,* a flat cake prepared from a mixture of manioc flour with water and coconut milk.[3] While serving as a pretext for Flor's reflections on the great variety of human tastes (*bolo de puba* and sex are the only two things that both husbands relish), the note ironically provides pseudo-documentation of her real-life existence.

A menu of the refreshments to be served at wakes appropriately prefaces the opening section of the novel, which treats of the death and life of Flor's first mate, the voluptuary Vadinho, along with the various exequial rites that must be observed (*Dona Flor,* 19–20). Prepared by the cooking teacher in response to a pupil's query, it stresses the essentiality of *cachaça* (white rum), be the decedent rich or poor. "A wake without cachaça shows a lack of consideration for the deceased, suggests indifference and contempt" (*Dona Flor,* 20).

The sensual delights of food and sex combine with a recipe for *moqueca de siri mole* (a ragout containing soft-shell crab meat) to introduce the story's second part (*Dona Flor,* 53–54). Formulated as one of Flor's cooking lessons, it is phrased in a loose poetic structure interspersed with the protagonist's silent recollections of her departed Vadinho. Inasmuch as this food had been the latter's favorite dish, some of the ingredients and directions vividly call to mind both the pleasure he derived from its preparation and consumption and the joy she received from the lips and mouth he used to devour it. "His teeth bit into the crab meat, / his lips were yellow with dendê oil. / Alas, never again his lips, / his tongue, never again / his mouth burning with raw onion!" (*Dona Flor,* 54).

Flor's class discussion of gourmet delicacies (turtle chowder, stewed lizard, and roast peccary) supplies still another opportunity for the author to juxtapose the joys of the palate with those of the flesh (*Dona Flor,* 209–10). After discoursing on her culinary recommendations for special occasions, the protagonist offers herself as the most succulent pièce de résistance:

> But if your guest wants even choicer, finer game, if he seeks the *ne plus ultra,* the ultimate, the last word, the pleasure of the gods, then why not serve him a widow, young and pretty, cooked in her tears of grief and loneliness, in the sauce of her modesty and mourning, in the moans of her bereavement, in the flame of her forbidden desire, which gives her the flavor of guilt and sin? Oh, I know of such a widow, of hot pepper and honey, cooking over a slow fire every night, just ready to be served. (*Dona Flor,* 209)

It is in this, the third, section of the narrative, that she is again to enter into holy wedlock. Yet only after the desperation and temptation

foreshadowed in the above lecture does this socially acceptable opportunity to satiate her hunger for male companionship materialize.

The final such insert, ostensibly prepared by Flor's *comadre*, Dionísia
de Oxóssi, is in effect the menu of the anthropomorphic *candomblé* gods
(*Dona Flor*, 395–96). Introducing the last section, wherein Vadinho's
permanent resurrection will be determined, it catalogues the prandial
preferences and dislikes of the various *orixás* (divinities), comically depicting their mortallike choosiness. "Omolu cannot stand shrimp."
"Oxóssi . . . is very picky . . . he won't eat fish without scales; he
can't tolerate yam and white beans" (*Dona Flor*, 395). Perhaps of more
significance to the story and its moral, sexual, and sociosatirical implications, though, are the observations concerning the patron saints
of Flor's two husbands. The Apollonian Teodoro, her second mate, is
protected by Oxalá, who in Bahia is associated with Nosso Senhor do
Bonfim (Jesus Christ). The Dionysian Vadinho is, on the other hand,
guarded by Exu, the mischievous orixá of orientation and disorienta-
tion, whom many believers equate with Lucifer, the fallen angel.
"Oxalá does not like seasonings; he does not use salt or tolerate oil"
(*Dona Flor*, 395). "For Exu, food is anything that he can get in his
mouth. But he drinks only one thing: pure cachaça" (*Dona Flor*, 396).

Certainly the most extensive use of recipes in the novel is in the
chapter "Apelo de Dona Flor em aula e em devaneio" (*Dona Flor*, 265–
68; Dona Flor's Appeal in Class and in Reverie), which occurs prior to
Teodoro's marriage proposal. Here, a lesson on how to prepare *vatapá*—
a combination of fish or chicken with dried shrimp, seasoned with
coconut milk, peanuts, cashews, ginger, hot peppers, and dendê palm
oil—is cleverly laced with the teacher's solemn pleas in reverie for a
marriage prospect to deliver her from the temptation to illicitly put an
end to her sexual famine. Certain words and parts of her explanation
provoke the alternating lascivious thoughts that plague her. Upon
mentioning that the best cooking oil, from Greece, is hard to find, she
is reminded of the awesome difficulty of finding a new partner. "If I
find a fiancé, what will I do?" (*Dona Flor*, 266). A suggestion that her
students not spare any elbow grease in grating the coconuts prompts
her to make an amusing mental observation: "They say that exercise
prevents evil thoughts; I don't believe it" (*Dona Flor*, 266). Once one
has finished the grating, the useless scraps (*bagaço*) may be thrown out,
she advises, musing that *bagaço* is really all that society considers a
widow to be (*Dona Flor*, 267). When all is properly mixed and finally
cooked over a low flame, she concludes, the dish is at last ready to be
eaten by one's husband or fiancé. The *fogo lento* in which her dreams

consume her, however, makes it ever more imperative that she find that fiancé to save her from "dishonor" and "perdition" (*Dona Flor,* 268). She, too, is ready to be "served." If the ginger, peppers, and peanuts, so essential to the *vatapá,* are commonly regarded as aphrodisiacs, she has never needed this dish or similar foods to awaken the drives that now threaten to destroy her reputation (*Dona Flor,* 267).

At times during the foregoing sequences the semantic levels of eating (food) and sex become so closely intertwined that dietary habits may be said to serve as metaphors for sexual behavior. Such a relationship is hinted at in Flor's early letter to the novelist (*Dona Flor,* 15) by the linking of *bolo de puba* and sexual intercourse. The analogy is further developed in the *moqueca* recipe (*Dona Flor,* 53–54). Here, by substituting the female body or Flor herself for the dish in question and sexual union for Vadinho's gormandizing, one obtains a much more graphic reading of Flor's recollections of her husband's "eating" pleasures than would otherwise have been produced. The interrelationship between the two levels of coherence goes beyond the four-term homology of eating–food–copulating–female. Indeed, both here and elsewhere, one is tempted to equate eating with copulation, food with female, and eater with male.[4]

So evident are these sexual overtones in Flor's menu suggestions for special occasions (*Dona Flor,* 209–10) that they need not be reiterated. Yet here, too, the implied metaphor *comer* is intensified if we keep in mind the word's semantic binarity in Brazil: "to eat" and "to copulate." This dual meaning may also be seen to underlie the continued equation of female and food in the later "Apelo" sequence (*Dona Flor,* 265–68). Only the wake menu (*Dona Flor,* 19–20) appears to have no significant connection with sexual referents.

It is in the bill of fare of the *orixás* (*Dona Flor,* 395–96) that the eating-sex metaphor is most explicitly used to polarize the personal and class features of the two spouses. Oxalá's aversion to all condiments and seasonings is clearly intended to be read as denoting the monotony and insipidness of Teodoro's sexual performances. Exu's lack of food biases is likewise meant to be a statement of Vadinho's sexual promiscuity. The social implications are obvious. Dietary and sexual contrasts may be regarded as paradigmatic of the intolerance/tolerance or regimentation/freedom oppositions that the novelist identifies with the middle-class-lower-class dichotomy. But what, then, does he gain by using this roundabout method of class portrayal instead of a more straightforward approach?

I have earlier suggested that the very unusualness (absurdity) of employing eating and sexual habits as class indicators accounts in some measure for their success. The humor surrounding the food-sex analogy performs a similar function. Class differences are formulated not as a life-and-death struggle, but in a tone of levity, which is much less threatening to the reader and thus more potentially palatable.

There is also another reason. Flor herself does not view her two husbands in terms of their socioeconomic origins or class-bound features, but rather principally in connection with their contrasting eating and sexual behaviors. In this regard she finds good and bad points in both of them. It is Vadinho, however, who comes out the winner, for of the two he is plainly the more closely identified with the pleasures of food and sex.

Amado's use of flavorful popular cookery to symbolize the simple yet epicurean habits of the lower classes thus strikes a satirical blow at the artificiality of abstinence and puritanism, so often imposed by polite society on the individual. It is by no means a ringing endorsement of the traditional counterculture's vices, however. Nor is it a condemnation of middle-class virtues. For Flor's ultimate solution to her dilemma—a magical combination of the best of both worlds—only goes to show that no one man, self-indulgent bohemian or "respectable" bourgeois, is capable of fulfilling her every need.

When forced to deny her sensual self by the fortunes of mortal life and the rigid mores of her community, Flor attempts to sublimate that facet of her being in the exercise of her culinary talents. Ironically, the two—food and sex—go hand in hand in the makeup of her personality,[5] a point that the author has repeatedly stressed through his equation of the two semantic planes. The preparation of tantalizing dishes is a constant reminder of the joys of lovemaking. The savory recipes and menus employed by the novelist, along with the abundant sexual episodes to which they often refer, represent an amusing paean to the wholesome pursuits of a life unshackled by false and unnatural restraints.

Roman à Clef Characters, a New Dimension

The introduction of real-life characters into the novel is one of the hallmarks of the mature Amado, as is the intensified climate of humor, irony, and satire to which it contributes. Literally hundreds of real individuals have been portrayed in the author's recent fiction, giving rise to an "in-group" brand of humor. It is my purpose here to examine the procedures by which this in-group humor is achieved, in an effort to clarify some of its narrative functions and satirical implications.

According to Paulo Tavares, author of a dictionary of Amadian characters, *Criaturas de Jorge Amado,* the novelist's characters as of 1979 numbered some 4,372, of which 802 (some 18 percent) existed or had existed in reality.[6] In other words, approximately eighteen per cent of Amado's "fictional" personages had been borrowed from the domain traditionally reserved to the genres of history and biography. Such data can be misleading, however, unless we are also aware of the distribution of such personages. Only in *Dona Flor* (1966) did Amado began to incorporate real figures into his fiction in any great numbers—a full thirty-five years after the publication of his first novel. True, a few of the author's friends appear in the novels prior to *Gabriela,* as well as in *Gabriela* itself, *Quincas, Comandante,* and *Pastores,* but they constitute only a small percentage of the total number of dramatis personae in any one of these works. This is not the case, however, with *Dona Flor,* where almost half of the 316 characters are drawn from reality.[7] Indeed, *Dona Flor e seus dois maridos* seems to have set a precedent. For in several of the author's subsequent novels, many of his intimates and associates have turned up alongside the cast of fictional figures, albeit in somewhat smaller numbers.

Although most of Amado's real-life characters have been relegated to brief appearances or minor roles,[8] some of the main characters of *Dona Flor* are quite clearly recognizable figures from the streets of Salvador, Bahia. In most cases their names have not been changed. Such characters, for example, are Dona Norma, who plays a major supporting role, Zé Sampaio, Dona Gisa, Bernabó, Tia Lita, and Tio Porto.[9] In fact, so many of the frontline personages of *Dona Flor* are based on Amado's friends that *Time* magazine, in a 1969 review of the English translation, was moved to comment, "According to rumor, Dona Flor's friends are not the Bahian poor, but Amado's own circle of artists and intellectuals, whom he has costumed as peasants for a literary romp *à clé.* To that degree, *Dona Flor* is a long, savory inside joke. It is not, however, malicious."[10]

Dona Flor and, to a lesser extent, some of Amado's other later works might be said to qualify as romans à clef, although not in the sense that they are satires on contemporary public figures whom the author disguises through caricature and fictitious names.[11] Rather, they adhere to the wider definition of "a novel that represents historical events and characters under the guise of fiction."[12] Amado tends to use the characters' real names, and although they may appear as caricatures, he normally pokes fun at them in a sympathetic, noncritical manner.

Even though the Amadian roman à clef usually does not disguise its characters, much of its humor is still confined to an in-group audience.[13] Amado's characters à clef are not as a rule the high and mighty. Some are indeed widely known within domestic and international artistic or literary circles, but most are not. Any comical or satirical effects intended by the author to derive from the presence of real persons in his fiction will thus be esoteric, escaping all but the particular real-life figures in question and that relatively small group of people who know them or know of them. The "key" to Amado's roman à clef is not to be found in history books.

Amadian in-group humor is based largely on fictional displacements, or deformations of reality, and the incongruities they produce. The most notable displacements are the following:

Juxtaposition of Real-Life Figures with Fictional (or Even Mythical or Supernatural) Figures

A case in point may be found in the wedding scene of *Tereza Batista,* where flesh-and-blood characters such as Amado's close friend José Mirabeau Sampaio, the Bahian singer-composer Caetano Veloso, and the novelist's wife Zélia Gattai[14] rub elbows with the call-girl protagonist and her prostitute friends (*Tereza,* 455–58). A comic effect is induced by the incongruity and surprise resulting from such an assemblage, which tends to blur the boundary between fantasy and objective reality. On the one hand, the real-life existence of purely fictional characters is ironically documented by their association with real individuals. On the other hand, the real individuals in question are, because of the particular fictional figures with whom they associate, immortalized in what the author considers to be a positive light—as simple folk, opposed to hypocrisy and concerned with the underprivileged.

An even more ludicrous instance of the device occurs in *Dona Flor.* Not only are inside characters such as Mirandão, Arigof, and Giovanni Guimarães[15] depicted as gambling partners of the fictional Vadinho; following the latter's untimely death, they are all privileged to receive betting tips from his rompish ghost (*Dona Flor,* 422–27, 440–46, 454–56).

Caricature of Real-Life Figures Exaggerated, even incongruous imitation of a real person's prominent physical traits, typical gestures, speech mannerisms, eccentricities, ruling passions, and the like may create a partial or comically grotesque picture of that person, especially when done at the expense of other, less noticeable characteristics. Repeated references are made to the ashen complexion of artist Jenner Augusto (*Dona Flor,* 116, 140, 181). Carlos Mascarenhas, later to become a noted politician, is distinguished time and again by his slender, beanpole-like profile (*Dona Flor,* 21, 116). Cardoso e Sª, a self-styled mystic and communicator with extraterrestrial beings, has as his trademark a rather unearthly guffaw (*Dona Flor,* 462, 463, 464, 482, 489, 494).[16] And Zé Sampaio is remembered as a stay-at-home hypochondriac with a strange habit of sucking his thumb (*Dona Flor,* 32, 33, 39, 181, 194, 218, 257, 258, 375).[17]

Yet the process need not involve leitmotif or incremental repetition within the text itself. Thus, caricature may also be seen in *Tereza Batista* in the depiction of the novel's illustrator, Calasans Neto, telling his joke about the whale for the one thousandth time (*Tereza,* 457), or in *Dona Flor* in the publisher, Barros Martins, dancing the tango at Salvador's Pálace Hotel on the night of Flor's birthday:[18]

The older and blacker [of a singing duet consisting of two sisters] had as her partner a tall, romantic type, dressed in the latest style, who had the look of a South American movie idol, the air of a gigolo. Vadinho later learned, when he was introduced to him, that he was from São Paulo on a visit to Bahia, Barros Martins by name, a respectable book publisher, and, of course, being a publisher, very rich. He was a whiz at the tango, with the air and competence of a professional, tracing letters, as they say, in an impeccable performance of the most intricate steps. (*Dona Flor,* 196)

Atypical or Out-of-Character Characterization A comical effect may be produced by the incongruity between a character's fictional role, identity, actions, or habits and those he or she possesses in real life. Such is the case of Bahian attorney and restaurateur Tibúrcio Barreiros,[19] who appears variously characterized in *Pastores, Dona Flor,* and *Tereza Batista.* Interviewed for a 1973 *Manchete* article, Barreiros stated that he preferred his role as a ukelele player in *Pastores* to the other two, even though he had never played the instrument in his life.[20] In *Gabriela,* Mário Cravo, the celebrated sculptor and close friend of Amado's, is relegated to the status of an "eccentric crafter of holy images, and a marketplace magician" (*Gabriela,* 433), while in *Tereza Batista* the late folklorist Luís da Câmara Cascudo is identified as a renowned grass-roots rhymester (*Tereza,* 99).[21]

Anachronism   Humor and irony may also arise from deliberate anachronism. Here, a comic effect is generated by circumstances similar to those involved in the juxtaposition of real with fictional figures: an element of playful surprise results from the temporal incongruity. One example of this process may be observed in *Tenda dos Milagres* in the appearance of poet Caetano Gil after the publication of one of Pedro Archanjo's books in 1928 (*Tenda,* 168). Granted, the character is a composite of two real individuals—Bahian entertainers Caetano Veloso and Gilberto Gil[22]—but a certain jestful incongruity stems from the fact that neither of the composite's donors had even been born at the time in question.

The technique is better illustrated perhaps by the case of Waldeloir Rego, born 1930, who in *Tenda* is placed back at the turn of the century (*Tenda,* 92, 158, 338), or in that of former Salvador mayor Epaminondas dos Santos Torres, who, though he died in 1955, is portrayed in *Comandante* as the renowned attorney who stole first prize from the story's fictional narrator in an academic contest presumably occurring around 1960 (*Comandante,* 170).[23]

Still more dramatic are the numerous instances of deliberate anachronism encountered in *Dona Flor.* Although the story apparently takes place between 1925 and 1935, there appear as adults at least fifteen real-life figures who were born after 1929. While Dr. Otaviano Pimenta,[24] a Bahian physician who died in 1942, is depicted as hosting Flor and Teodoro on their wedding night in Paripe (*Dona Flor,* 305), Marilda Alves,[25] an actress who was not born until 1946, is shown working as an apprentice to Flor before Teodoro's marriage proposal (*Dona Flor,* 215). Moreover, one of Amado's boyhood friends, Giovanni Guimarães, who died in 1966, appears with his wife and baby daughter Ludmila,[26] born 1957, around the time of Vadinho's ghostly resurrection—still supposedly within the 1925–35 time frame (*Dona Flor,* 455).[27] Further examples abound. The technique of anachronism, like the initial juxtaposition device, is more than a simple comic ploy to excite laughter through incongruity. It is, in fact, a form of fictional condensation, which the novelist uses to reduce the human landscape of a lifetime to a few essential personalities. As such, it constitutes a subversion and transformation of the empirical world.

Nostalgia   In *Dona Flor, Tenda,* and *Tereza Batista,* the fact that the stories occur some years ago, depicting particular real persons as they were or might well have been, but have long since ceased to be, adds a decidedly comical dimension to the narrative. It has been claimed that oftentimes humor = tragedy + time + distance. Certainly, too, situations, circumstances, ideas, and styles that at some time in our lives we have taken seriously often become laughable with the passage of time. Thus the depiction of Dorival Caymmi in *Dona Flor* as a young, struggling musician (116–19) is comically incongruous to those of us who have known him or known of him only as an immortal in the history of Brazilian popular music.[28] Even the great were not always so great, Amado seems to be saying—they were once younger and perhaps more frivolous. Nostalgia, then, is rather a distortion performed by the reader, not by the writer. Yet, it is the latter who consciously induces the process.

Dissociation   The portrayal of a real-life figure as two or more separate fictional characters in the same book, each representing a different facet of his or her personality, can generate considerable ironic humor. This technique is especially effective when the figure is known by two different names, has a multifaceted personality or field of activities, or has undergone some important transition that divides his or her life into two parts. Such is the case of the Argentine-born artist Héctor Julio Páride Bernabó,[29] who adopted the name Carybé when he moved to Salvador. At one point in *Dona Flor* the painter Carybé comes to talk over some business with the highly ethnocentric Argentine ceramicist Bernabó. An argument soon arises over the relative superiority or inferiority of the tango to the samba, causing Carybé to lose his temper and say of Argentina: "A country where there are no mulattas, all lily-white, is no place for anyone to live. Come off it!" (*Dona Flor,* 259). Thus is witnessed a fictional debate between the artist's Argentine self and his Brazilian self, the psychodrama of his dual nature.

Similar is the portrayal of José Mirabeau Sampaio,[30] the Bahian doctor, artist, professor, and shoe merchant, whom we have earlier encountered. He too plays a dual role in *Dona Flor.* He is fictionalized not only as Zé Sampaio, the homebody and imaginary invalid married

to the ebullient Dona Norma, but also as Zequito Mirabeau, the confirmed bohemian and ladies' man, known throughout Bahian whore-
dom for his adonic beauty:

One of the few times he [Zé Sampaio] had been there [Salvador's Pálace Ho-
tel], dragged against his will by Dona Norma . . . an unpleasant incident
had occurred. Mr. Sampaio had only left the table for a moment, out of a
pressing need to use the rest room, when a wiseacre had come along and tried
to strike up a conversation with Dona Norma, inviting her to dance and
complimenting her on her dress and eyes, as if she were just anybody. The
only reason Mr. Sampaio had not made an example of the rogue was that he
knew his family, his mother, Dona Belinha, and his two sisters, very distinguished people, excellent customers of his, and also the scoundrel himself, an
inveterate gambler and bohemian, Zequito Mirabeau, also known among the
harlots as "Mirabeau the beautiful." (*Dona Flor,* 195)

Association   The opposite of the above dissociation is also seen
where Amado combines, or associates, two or more figures from reality,
lumping them together into a composite fictional personage. This may
be done to stress the similarities of personality, action, behavior, or
contribution of two well-known figures. As we have seen, the author
employs such a device in *Tenda,* introducing a composite character and
giving him a composite name, Caetano Gil, in order to underscore the
oneness and harmony of the artistic accomplishments of Bahian com-
poser-musicians Caetano Veloso and Gilberto Gil (*Tenda,* 168). In this
particular circumstance, the humor derives more from the incongruity
of the hybrid name than from the combination of the two individuals,
as it does also with the character Floriano Coelho, who is synthesized
from the names of the novelist's two artist friends Floriano Teixeira and
Fernando Coelho[31] (*Tenda,* 79).
    The technique may also be used to create a fresh fictional character
out of the disparate qualities of several real human models, shifting the
emphasis from the personality and achievements of the latter individuals to those of the former. Thus the character's name may provide no
clues to the identity of the donors, and any resulting humor will necessarily be strongly esoteric.[32] A good example of this device is Pedro
Archanjo, the protagonist of *Tenda,* who, according to Amado, is actually a composite of at least three real-life figures: Manuel Querino,
Martiniano do Bonfim, and Miguel Arcanjo Santana.[33] Although
Amado has used for the works of Pedro Archanjo paraphrased versions

of some of the actual titles of Querino's monographs, he sees irony in the fact that Querino, a black sociologist, attempted to dissociate himself from the lower classes, an attitude inconsistent with the personality of the fictional Archanjo. "Querino moved upward," says Amado, but "Pedro Archanjo moved forward."[34] Humor and irony are also produced by the incongruity many middle-class readers would find in a *candomblé* priest's educating himself and in his teaching of French, German, and Spanish. But this is precisely what happened with *babalaô* Martiniano do Bonfim, who was giving a foreign-language lesson on the day Amado first met him, and on whom these traits in Pedro Archanjo were based. And it is to the fame of Miguel Santana as a ladies' man that one may attribute the sex appeal and amorous prowess of Archanjo. Santana was long a leader in the Axé Opô Afonjá *candomblé*, of which Amado is a dignitary.

Disguise   Real-life characters in Amado's books are occasionally disguised. The change of name of a real-life character—especially if the character remains recognizable through conventional associations— may itself be humorous. Thus Major Damião de Souza of *Tenda* is readily identifiable as the late Bahian people's lawyer Major Cosme de Farias (*Tenda,* 44 and passim).[35] The Catholic saints Cosme and Damian were twin brothers, and neither is generally spoken of in Brazil without mentioning the other. It should be noted, however, that here we laugh not only at the caricature of the real individual, but also—maybe even more—at the disguise itself. It is so transparent for the connoisseur of Bahia as to seem absurd.

Another example of the device is Argileu Palmeira, the itinerant poet of *Gabriela,* whose flamboyant calling card identifies him as "bachelors" (*Gabriela,* 305ff.). He was inspired by the peripatetic bard Argileu Silva, who, according to Amado, had such a *cartão de visita,* since he possessed not one but two academic degrees.[36]

Geographical Dislocation   The transference of real-life figures from their actual environments to new locales is another practice used sparingly by Amado, and one from which only very few will derive any measure of humor. An out-of-place characterization of sorts is evidenced in *Dona Flor,* where the novelist assembles his friends on Salvador's Rua do Sodré, as if they had all lived there together at one time. This was never the case in reality, however.[37]

More noteworthy perhaps is the characterization of João Fulgêncio,

Nhô Galo, and Capitão Miguel Batista de Oliveira of *Gabriela,* who are based on persons Amado knew in the town of Estância, Sergipe (*Gabriela,* 32, 36 ,37, and passim). For purposes of the novel, he has transported them all to Ilhéus, Bahia.[38] Like the technique of anachronism, geographical dislocation thus allows the novelist to condense the real world, violating its material constraints in order to create a tighter, more compact fictional universe.

Anonymous Characterization   Perhaps the most infrequent and also the most restricted of the novelist's in-group displacements is what might be called anonymous characterization, or namelessness. An early instance of this takes place in *Terras do sem fim,* where the small boy chosen by the judge to draw the names of prospective jurors during the courtroom trial of Col. Horácio da Silveira is none other than Amado himself as a child (*Terras,* 279–84).

More comical, though, is the appearance in *Tenda* of an unnamed footwear magnate, referred to only as "the Client" (*Tenda,* 139–40). Of course, this is again José Mirabeau Sampaio. Those who know him or have seen pictures of him will not fail to identify him as the "man in his fifties with bushy eyebrows, wearing a school ring." For besides this unmistakable physical description and several mentions of the actual company name (Casas Stela), there follows a portrayal of the client as an aficionado of antiques, a quality to which Mirabeau's large collection of religious figurines gives him ample claim.

No doubt there are other fictional displacements that contribute to the author's in-group humor; those listed above are but some of the most visible. A more exhaustive study of the topic would find that many specific episodes where inside characters are involved are actually based on real or rumored events. One need not go to that length, however, in order to draw some conclusions as to the narrative role and satirical purpose of these characters à clef.

One common denominator seems to be a homogenization or leveling effect. The mimetic mode of portrayal that invests much of Amadian, and indeed Western, fiction with a semblance—but *only* a semblance—of the real world is drawn ever closer to history and the empirical universe by the intrusion of historical figures.[39] Fictional characters, by association, are thus made to seem more living than lifelike, more veridical than verisimilar. For their part, the flesh-and-blood intruders, once removed from the material universe, escape their condition of mortality, but in so doing forfeit their organic unity. They become partial, burlesque images of themselves. In a word, they move from the historical toward the fictional. All the more so when Amado gleefully places them side by side with deities or ghosts.

Thus is produced, through the agency of in-group humor, an intermediate world—not quite fact, not quite fiction—where reality and imagination coalesce. Within this magical middle ground, in-group humor techniques are free to dismount and reassemble the material universe to conform more closely to the author's ideals. Hence their wish-fulfillment function. Barriers of time and place are made to vanish. Worlds are compressed. Death and aging lose their finality. Individuals are reborn, combined, divided. Amado attempts to replace what is with what ought to be.

This brings us to the satirical ramifications of in-group humor. There is no denying that a great deal of it is indeed without significant personal or social criticism. But that does not mean that it is merely pointless jest; only that it is primarily intended to entertain in the teasing manner of a lively but inoffensive private joke. *Dona Flor* is known to have upset a few of the individuals immortalized in its pages; one critic has even called it "the Satiricon of local life."[40] Over the years Amado has also had his share of angry denunciations and lawsuits from persons who thought they saw themselves depicted in his characters.[41] Yet the great majority of those fictionalized have seemed more flattered than insulted.

The reasons for this are simple. Not only are such characters usually treated with playful irony rather than ridicule, but for all their quirks and inconsistencies, they are repeatedly shown to stand on the side of social justice, to befriend the less fortunate, and to oppose pretension and hypocrisy. Moreover, they are often shown to reject the worst values of their particular social groups, though perhaps still displaying one or more of the latter's class-bound eccentricities. Thus there emerges not the ad hominem satire often associated with the roman à clef, but a social satire of classes and customs.

It is clear that Amado employs in-group characters and humor for much more than mere decorative reasons. The comic stylization techniques by which he incorporates real individuals into the text as bonafide fictional personages serve to unite, transform, and satirize the disparate tiers of reality that thus come into play. Fiction and fact are meshed; real beings transcend the confines of the workaday world. Amado's in-group characters are stripped of their social masks and costumed as champions of justice and truth.

To unlock the Amadian roman à clef is thus to share the tolerant smile with which the novelist sees the foibles and passions of his own group of friends. It is also to discover a rich, new dimension in his satirical view of the world.

The Afro-Brazilian Gods—Agents of Apocalypse and Redemption?

Unquestionably, the greatest departure from documentary realism in Amado's later works lies in the increasing intervention of the Afro-Brazilian supernatural in the lives of his characters. For all the criticism it has provoked from some of the admirers of his earlier, overtly political fiction, the novelist's conversion to so-called magic realism has probably done more to enhance his ideological message than to diminish it. The satirical implications of this latter-day preference for otherworldly solutions to human imbroglios stem from the wish-fulfillment role usually played by such "miracles." Redress of social injustice no longer rests with the Brazilian Communist party or with any particular political ideology, but ironically with a pantheon of anthropomorphic divinities whose existence Amado, a confirmed materialist, rejects from other than a symbolic viewpoint.[42]

Some of the comic ramifications of such extramundane meddling in human affairs derive from the apparent superstition and naïveté of the characters involved. In *Pastores,* Negro Massu's initial vision of Ogum, for example, may be just as plausibly explained as a figment of his imagination. What matters, though, is not its reality or irreality, but that it eventually leads to a solution to his problem of choosing a godfather for his infant son (*Pastores,* 152). Much of the humor connected with such divine intercession, though, has to do with its role as an agent of redemption and retribution for the social underdog in the absence of viable earthly relief. This is particularly true in *Dona Flor* and *Tereza Batista.* Only in death is Vadinho able to defeat his archnemesis, the roulette wheel, by repeatedly rigging it to stop on his favorite number for a selected group of friends. (*Dona Flor,* 422–27, 440–46, 454–56). Tereza Batista and friends are rescued time and again from injustice or imminent danger by Oxalufá (old Oxalá), who appears in the form of a mysterious old man wearing a beard and white suit and carrying a gold cane (*Tereza,* 357, 398, 432, 443, 449). In *Tereza Batista,* even the Brazilian romantic poet Antônio de Castro Alves (1847–71) is resurrected to aid the striking harlots against police brutality (*Tereza,* 436), while one high-ranking police officer falls to the street and breaks both legs supposedly in punishment of his dese-cration of an altar dedicated to the prankish Exu (*Tereza,* 427, 443).

The ascription of human traits and vices to the various Afro-Brazil-ian deities, the *orixás,* constitutes a fertile source of humor in the later fiction. This is very much in line with the traditional portrayals of the Yoruban supernatural. "Like the Greek gods, the Yoruba orishas are deeply involved in the affairs of humans when they are not preoccupied with their own affairs," observes Harold Courlander in his *Tales of the Yoruba Gods and Heroes.* "Their virtues or vanities are human attributes raised to godly stature; and they can be fallible, arbitrary or whimsical in their attitudes and actions . . . the orishas have amoral characters."[43] Thus in *Pastores* several Afro-Brazilian divinities are shown to exhibit mortal-like arrogance and obstinacy (185). And in *Tereza Batista* some of the male *orixás* are said to have sexual relations with their respective female votaries (42, 366, 415).

Exu is by far the most roguish of the *candomblé* spirits depicted in Amado's fiction. Often associated in popular belief with Satan, he is both worshiped and feared for his reputed ability to wreak havoc on those who ignore his powers, whims, and saintly guidance. Forever lurking at the crossroads of space and time, Exu, it is said, may either show the correct way to life's travelers or sidetrack them with his ample supply of devilish tricks. Hence the need to humor him, to initiate all *candomblé* rites by tendering his customary propitiatory offering. In their haste to christen the son of Negro Massu, the faithful in *Pastores* apparently forget to do so and thus become the target of one of his pranks (*Pastores,* 194, 195). Ogum (another *orixá*), decides to become the child's godfather, and although the decision saves Massu from hav-ing to decide which one of his friends to select for the honor, it creates a serious obstacle: the officiating Catholic priest would certainly not allow a *candomblé* spirit to serve in that capacity. To avoid any difficulty with the church, a devotee of Ogum is chosen to represent the *orixá* in the baptismal ritual; the problem appears to be solved. However, those in attendance who are privy to the mysteries of *candomblé* immediately spot something out-of-character in the behavior of the stand-in: the exaggerated dance steps, the stubbornness, the Homeric laughter, and the utter shamelessness. Ogum has been delayed, and it is Exu who has taken possession of the substitute and is sowing chaos. Thus, once the impostor has disclosed his true identity, even the real Ogum must resort to human devices when, in order to foil his colleague's scampish interference, he momentarily takes charge of the body and brain of the unwitting priest. To the uninitiated, the spectacle of a man of the cloth's slapping the face of the godfather-to-be during a christening ritual must be a strange sight indeed. But to those conversant with *candomblé* affairs it is merely part of the ongoing shenanigans in which the *orixás* are wont to indulge (*Pastores,* 186–96).

Both the political symbolism and the satirical connotations with which the novelist frequently invests the Afro-Brazilian supernatural are most evident in the antics of Exu. Selfish though he often seems, this lord of anarchy rarely fails to protect his votaries. Of the several latter-day Amadian protagonists who display a rogue's disdain for society's regimentation and hypocrisy, *Dona Flor*'s Vadinho is particularly identified with Exu, whom he is said to regard as his patron saint. In fact, among the immortals, Exu proves to be his only advocate in his struggle to retain his ghostly presence in the young widow's bed. All of the other deities, led by Yansã, favor his demise. The resulting clash, reminiscent of the theomachies of Greek epic, succeeds in unleashing a series of strange cataclysmic events:

The city rose up in the air and the clocks showed midnight and noon at the same time in the war of the gods. All the orixás had come to bury Vadinho, the rebellious spirit of the dead, and his burden of love, with only Exu to defend him. Lightning and thunder, storm, steel against steel, and black blood. . . .

Then the maidens of the city undressed themselves and went out to offer themselves in the streets and public squares. Then the children were born, by the thousands. All alike, for they were all the children of Vadinho, all awkward and perverse. Out to sea sailed houses and mansions, the Barra lighthouse and the manor house of Unhão; the Fortress of the Sea was transported to the Terreiro de Jesus, and fish sprouted in the gardens and stars ripened in the trees. The Palace clock marked the hour of terror in a crimson sky with yellow spots.

Then a dawn of comets began to shine above the brothels, and every harlot received a husband and children. The moon shone upon Itaparica above the mangrove swamps, and the lovers picked it up, and in its mirror kisses and swoons were reflected. . . .

The people came running down the hillsides with kerosene lances and a calendar of strikes and revolts. When they got to the square, they set fire to the dictatorship as if it were a piece of dirty paper and lighted freedom on every corner.

It was the Devil who led the revolt, and at ten thirty-six in the evening order and feudal tradition came crashing to the ground. Of conventional morality there remained only the broken pieces, and these were gathered up and taken to the Museum. (*Dona Flor,* 493–94)

Such apocalyptic occurrences probably come the closest of anything in the novel to conveying Amado's sociopolitical intentions and explaining the symbolism of his heroine. The conflict between the various *orixás* is viewed by the author as a symbolic clash between the forces of reaction and those of freedom. Thus the supernatural, ironically with a devil figure as its prime mover, serves in the end to redress the ills of society by acting out a symbolic wish fulfillment in which natural and social laws are playfully but violently rent asunder. The established order is chaotically overturned, not by some political party of right or left, but by a community of anthropomorphic divinities, whose existence is more poetic than real. What may seem desirable yet unattainable by empirical standards is ironically rendered feasible through the agency of playful, unrestrained fantasy.

Amado seems to be saying that the salvation of both the individual and society depends on human will and initiative as much as on this creative fantasy. For in the end it is not so much the efforts of the Yoruban divinities that bring about the novel's magical solution as it is the desire and determination of Dona Flor herself. In the war of the gods, Exu's support proves to be insufficient to protect the vanishing Vadinho from imminent extinction. All hope appears to be lost; Yansã and her cohorts have all but won. "When suddenly a figure traversed the air, and breaking through the most impenetrable paths, overcame both distance and hypocrisy—a thought free from all shackles. It was Dona Flor, in all her nakedness. Her cry of love drowned out Yansã's cry of death. . . . A blaze lit up the earth and the people set fire to the time of lies" (*Dona Flor,* 495).

If, as Joseph Campbell has claimed, "dream is the personalized myth, myth the depersonalized dream,"[44] then it stands to reason that myth, like the dreams of an individual, not only says a great deal about a people's aspirations and anxieties, but also seeks to compensate for the deficiencies and limitations of its station within society. In its acculturated and still-evolving form, African religion transplanted to Brazil has long been a defense against engulfment and oppression by the dominant European culture. As such, it has also functioned as a social escape valve with which the have-nots, mostly black and mulatto, have sublimated many of their hostilities toward the economic and cultural hegemony of the ruling classes. Magic and the supernatural have accordingly come to be taken by many as a normal component of everyday life. What Amado has thus tried to do with many of the aforementioned examples of divine intervention is to blend them into the texture of tangible reality, homogenizing the supernatural with the natural in such a way that one seems to be the logical extension of the other. Such a technique, which has been alleged by some critics to be a characteristic device of baroque literature,[45] comically underscores the tenuousness of the purely material and rational by placing them on the same plane as the spiritual and the irrational. In a word, it is difficult to decide just where one ends and the other begins. The reader is at times so adeptly drawn into the world of Amadian fantasy that, as in a dream, he or she too begins to take much of the absurdity in stride.

It can thus be argued that Amado's use of the Afro-Bahian supernatural performs not one but several functions. It not only serves to whet readers' interests by teasing their imaginations, but also seeks to inspire much-needed political and social reforms through implied or open ridicule of the status quo. It is often used to expose the relativity of truth or the inadequacy of purely rationalistic solutions. Moreover, it normally seeks to stress what the author seems to regard as the uniqueness and basic humanity of Afro-Brazilian culture. Far from serving to legitimize backwardness, then, Amado's introduction of the supernatural into his fiction may be seen as an artistic device symbolic of his dissatisfaction with the mundane, the confining, the unjust, and the hypocritical. Theurgical intervention in the affairs of the novelist's characters should thus not be read as an assertion of their need for dependence on otherworldly solutions or of the poor's powerlessness to change their lives, but rather, on the contrary, as an affirmation of the supremacy of human will and of the self-sufficiency of the Brazilian masses to effect their own solutions.

Chapter Six

Tereza Batista cansada de guerra: A *Cordel* Novel

A Tale of the Sordid and the Sublime

Tereza Batista cansada de guerra owes much of its appeal to the fact that its protagonist is drawn as a legendary heroine rather than a "realistic" or "mimetic" character. Tereza is the subject not only of several popular *cordel* ballads mentioned in the story, but also of the five *cordel* episodes, or *folhetos,* with which the novel itself is ostensibly structured. Throughout the various sections—each of which parodies the high-flown style of this formulaic poetry in several of its most characteristic features—Tereza seems to experience few of the psychological contradictions that one would expect of a modern novelistic heroine. Nor does she undergo any major changes as a character. For the most part she is static, opaque, and rather unidimensional from one cover to the other, not unlike many of the epic heroines and heroes of popular legend the world over.

As is the case with Flor, Amado goes to great lengths to document Tereza Batista's "real-life" existence right from the beginning of the novel. After dedicating the volume to his wife, Zélia, he proceeds in the guise of an authorial narrator to describe his last encounter with the heroine, with whom he juxtaposes a number of his close friends. All are said to have attended the fiftieth anniversary celebration of the religious investment of a famous Bahian *candomblé* priestess.[1] This is followed by the music and lyrics of a song supposedly written about Tereza Batista by popular composer Dorival Caymmi, another long-time friend of the novelist.[2] Like the preceding passage and a similar scene in the final episode of the novel, in which many of Amado's friends and family members are seen at Tereza's wedding reception (*Tereza,* 455–58), this item ironically serves to proclaim the heroine's flesh-and-blood existence, a kind of leveling effect being achieved with the juxtaposition.

A similar authenticating role is played by the first of two epigraphs that directly precede the narrative proper: "Plague, famine and war; death and love; Tereza Batista's life is a *cordel* story." Besides signaling the reader as to the novelist's parodic intentions, the line, which one presumes to be a quotation from some actual *folheto*, functions in much the same way as Borges's fictitious footnotes or the anonymous popular song used to introduce Amado's own *Gabriela, cravo e canela,* in that it makes specific reference to an allegedly existing text outside the present fictional universe, thus providing a kind of pseudo-documentation by pseudo-intertextuality of the protagonist's ontological status.

The "myth" of Tereza's real-life existence is perpetuated and further buttressed elsewhere in the novel by the author's use of a narrative frame in which he (or his persona, in the guise of an authorial narrator) serves to collect and weave together the various strands of her story, relying on the fragmentary and often contradictory accounts of popular informants, some of them real or historical figures, who intervene in the narrative from time to time to tell a particular incident in their own words.[3] The principal narrator begins his story as follows:

When they heard I was going back to those parts, they asked me to bring back word of Tereza Batista, to see if I could clear up a few matters. There's certainly no shortage of curious folks in the world; that's for sure.

So I nosed around here and there, in the open markets of backwoods towns and down on the waterfront, and after some time and initial distrust, managed to hear all the reports and accounts, some of them funny, others sad, that each person told in his own way and according to his particular knowledge. I pieced together everything I heard and could make sense of—fragments of stories, tunes played on the harmonica, dance steps, cries of despair and sighs of love, all mixed up and run together—and brought it back for all the people that wanted to know about the affairs and wanderings of that copper-hued girl. I don't have a lot to tell. People there are not all that talkative, and those that know the most say the least. Nobody wants to be certified as a genuine liar. (*Tereza,* before pagination)

To the extent, then, that this rather chatty, colloquial narrator is associated in the reader's mind with Amado himself, he too serves to affirm the reality of the heroine. It is these two elements—on the one hand, a claim of total or at least substantial factuality and, on the other (as we mentioned above), a declared artificiality (that of the *cordel* genre, of which the narrator is the presumed cultivator)—that most fundamentally underlie the work and mark the characterization of its female protagonist.

Both elements figure in the story itself. Stark realism is juxtaposed with the colorful and often contrived trappings of formulaic narrative. The sordid is often mixed with the sublime. Real-life characters are presented alongside fictional personages, and several divine and historical figures are summoned especially for the occasion.

Orphaned at the age of eight, Tereza Batista is sold to a rich Bahian *fazenda* owner by her aunt before reaching her thirteenth birthday. For the next two years she is forced to submit to the cruelest of physical abuses and sexual indignities by Capitão Justo, her perverted captor.[4] She is finally seduced by a handsome but cowardly student who, instead of delivering her, flees when the couple's intimacies are discovered. Thus, in order to avoid being summarily slain herself, Tereza thrusts a knife into the irate Captain's groin.

While awaiting trial for the "heinous murder," the fifteen-year-old is suddenly released from jail and placed in a convent, and all charges are dropped, thanks to the intercession of Dr. Emiliano Guedes, a local industrialist. But Tereza, unaware of the latter's efforts in her behalf and encouraged by the madam of a brothel, escapes her confinement and goes to work as a prostitute. Upon learning of this, Dr. Emiliano carries her away on horseback to the neighboring state of Sergipe, where he sets her up as his mistress in a country house. For the next six years Tereza lives in peace and satisfaction as the lover, ward, and protégée of an "enlightened monarch," who maintains her in comfort and gives her education and polish.

With Emiliano's death—which occurs while they are making love— she is again left, however, to fend for herself. First she becomes an entertainer in a dance hall in Aracaju, where she acquires a reputation of belligerence by defending a battered woman against her attacking lover. When next we see her she is leading an army of prostitutes into battle against a smallpox epidemic in the interior town of Buquim. And finally, when this is over we find her in Salvador, Bahia, where, while once again working as a dance-hall entertainer and part-time call girl, she leads a successful prostitutes' strike, defying the local authorities, who jail and beat her. It is here, too, that, following the settlement of the labor dispute, she again finds the love of her life, Januário Gereba, a sailor whom she had met in Aracaju and thought to be dead. The two are married and begin to plan a family. Thus ends Tereza's story, as fancifully as it began.

The sheer accumulation of realistic details in an episode such as that of Tereza's captivity and sexual abuse seems to have a dual and contradictory effect. On the one hand, such details help to assure the reader of the ultimate veracity of the occurrence. On the other hand, they tend, by virtue of their close association with and contamination by the elements of pure artifice and fantasy, to intensify the grotesqueness of the story. Much the same could be said of the smallpox episode, in which a plethora of distasteful particulars—not to mention the very lowness of the prostitute-heroines' social station—collides oxymoronically with the high-flown epic style. Likewise, there is a constant tension in an episode such as that of the prostitutes' strike created by the author's habit of injecting a heavy dose of coincidence, farcical humor, and the supernatural into an otherwise serious social struggle.

The Imprint of Popular Poetry

As for the novel's parody of *cordel* literature—its burlesque imitation of art, as opposed to nature—it may be seen, for example, in the use of long, enumerative section titles such as "The Girl Who Bled the Captain with a Jerky Knife," "ABC of Tereza Batista's Battle with the Black Smallpox," and "Tereza Batista's Debut at the Cabaret in Aracaju; or, Tereza Batista's Gold Tooth; or, Tereza Batista and the Punishment of the Usurer." The first of these is typical of the *folhetos* of the *exemplum* variety, particularly those that tell of violent or prodigious events. Mark Curran, in his study of *cordel* elements in Amado's fiction, cites two authentic examples of this tendency: *The Girl Who Beat Her Mother and Was Turned into a Dog* and *The Girl Who Danced with the Devil*.[5] The second title is characteristic of the many popular, often epic poems of modern-day Brazil whose successive stanzas begin with successive letters of the alphabet, from *A* to *Z*. The third example is representative of the tendency of some *cordel* poets to assign multiple, alternative titles to their works, as if to imitate the literature of bygone epochs. Each of the novel's section titles, in turn, appears as part of an illustrative woodcut, in which artist Calasans Neto, a good friend of the novelist, quite clearly imitates the often primitive xylographs that traditionally grace the covers of the *folhetos*.[6]

There are also other, less obvious imprints of *literatura de cordel* upon the novel and its protagonist. One involves the author's deliberate appropriation and adaptation of several specific plot motifs common to Brazilian and Iberian folk tradition. Candace Slater has traced the parallels between Tereza Batista and the *donzela guerreira*, or warrior maiden, of the Luso-Hispanic folk ballad.[7] She notes several similarities and differences of plot and character between the traditional *romance* (ballad) and the episode of the novel in which Tereza comes to the defense of the battered woman. Curran is reminded by the same episode of a *folheto* entitled *The Bold Deeds of a Backwoods Woman,* in which a woman struggles to defend herself. He also identifies several *cordel* poems as possible sources for some of the other episodes.[8] And Daphne Patai notes the apparent influence of such popular narratives as *Donzela Teodora* and *Princesa Magalona* on various parts of the novel.[9]

By far the most pervasive influence of *cordel* and other folk literature on the novel, though, is the ever-present hyperbolic tone that informs many of the episodes and characters. It is in this context, too, that we must consider the nonmimetic, legendary characterization of the novel's larger-than-life heroine. Certainly, there is something of this tendency toward overstatement in the humorous and sometimes wordy section titles discussed above. So, too, is there a great deal of caricatural exaggeration in the accompanying woodcuts. Episodes such as the battle with the smallpox epidemic and the victorious prostitutes' strike are elevated to epic proportions by the author's deliberate overstatement of the contrasting moral qualities attached to the two competing forces and by his virtual elimination of all moral ambiguities. The introduction of a pantheon of anthropomorphic divinities and the zoomorphic portrayal of the smallpox epidemic as a horrible monster serve a similar function. And characters such as Capitão Justo and Januário Gereba are infinitely more sinister or more heroic than any lifelike novelistic personage has the right to be.

By the same token the protagonist herself is hyperbolized far beyond any of the novelist's other characters. She is endowed with much greater strength, intelligence, and courage than the normal mimetic hero or heroine of most contemporary fiction could ever reasonably hope to display. Both her ordeals and adventures, too, are exaggerated, a direct result of her status as a *cordel* heroine. To be sure, she would appear to be more at home in a folk tale, classical legend, or medieval romance than in a novel. She is a unidimensional, static character, at times as enigmatic and inscrutable as any epic heroine; like the latter, she undergoes a new metamorphosis with the overcoming of each adversity and receives a new epithet for every triumph. She is at once "Tereza Favo-de-Mel" (Tereza Honeycomb) and "Tereza Boa de Briga" (Tereza the Fighter), "Tereza da Bexiga Negra" (Tereza of the Black Smallpox) and "Tereza Batista Cansada de Guerra" (Tereza Batista Weary of War). The list continues. Such new identities, rather than signaling any true multidimensionality or dynamism of character on Tereza's part, are superimposed on—not exchanged for—one another and merely serve to strengthen her superlative, monolithic nature. She can function convincingly only in a world of absolutes, exempt from the normal complexities of the material universe, an idealized fictional space in which virtue is ultimately rewarded and evil punished, where both heroic acts and villainy are greatly magnified.

Probably the least mimetic of the literary devices in *Tereza Batista* associated with the hyperbole of *cordel* poetry is that of the supernatural and divine intervention, or theurgy. The presence of werewolves, headless mules, and other such monsters, the heroine's frequent rescue by one voodoo divinity or another and the attribution to her of miraculous powers by several of the novel's secondary narrators are clearly intended by the author to recall the supernatural element as it exists in many a *folheto*. Like the heroes and heroines of Greco-Roman epic, *cordel* protagonists are frequently supplied with divine protection and their efforts aided or hindered by supernatural machinery, albeit normally of Christian rather than classical or African origin. Grotesque monsters, often deriving from Amerindian or African folk tales, as well as fabulous creatures, amulets, and other magical objects, which can be traced to Carolingian or earlier, Levantine sources, are likewise part of the *cordel* reader's literary experience.[10]

"The hero of romance," as Northrop Frye observes, "moves in a world in which the ordinary laws of nature are slightly suspended: prodigies of courage and endurance, unnatural to us, are natural to him, and enchanted weapons, talking animals, terrifying ogres and witches, and talismans of miraculous power violate no rule of probability once the postulates of romance have been established." He adds: "Here we have moved from myth, properly so called, into legend, folk tale, *märchen*, and their literary affiliates and derivatives."[11] It may thus be argued that by participating fully in this aspect of the *cordel* tradition, too, the present work and its heroine are much closer to the genre of romance than they are to the modern novel.

Yet not only do such elements serve to strengthen Tereza Batista's claim to being a *cordel* heroine, related to the protagonists of romance and legend, but in the end, they also underscore her connection to the mythical sorceress figure common to these genres. Unlike the witches and other assorted Terrible Mother characters often found in "naive" and formulaic literature, however, Tereza Batista is not merely the symbolic embodiment of danger and opposition to a traditionally male hero. She is a heroine in her own right, the protagonist of her own story, with her own constellation of helpers and antagonists. Nor is she the negative character that one would expect of a traditional witchlike figure. Quite the contrary. Although she may indeed constitute a threat to those characters whom the author brands as "oppressors," to those who perpetuate her feats in legend—the "little people," the victims of oppression—she is nothing less than a "benevolent witch," a popular heroine, whose extraordinary accomplishments set her above the common run of humanity and are worthy of imitation by all. Her sorcerous image and wondrous powers—indeed, the allegiance afforded her by the various Afro-Brazilian *orixás*—thus serve to further evoke her "literariness" at the expense of more mimetic lines of characterization, deriving as they do from an imitation of *cordel*'s marked propensity for overstatement.

Parody or Stylization?

Parody itself accounts for some of the novel's hyperbolic tenor. To the extent that it burlesques the conventions of *cordel* poetry, the style of *Tereza Batista* is a ludicrous exaggeration of something that is already itself ludicrously exaggerated. Patai claims that in *Tereza Batista* Amado in fact is not parodying popular literature at all, "but rather lovingly creating new versions of it, however contradictory this may appear." He indeed imitates the style of the *folheto,* but he does so engaging the reader's imagination in a traditional manner, she contends, "without directing irony toward the literary form from which he borrows, but rather with marked nostalgia."[12] This argument seems to invoke Bakhtin's and Tynianov's distinction between parody and stylization, the latter differing from the former in that it uncritically validates the conventions of the imitated work or genre rather than undermining or "demystifying" them.[13] There is no denying Amado's obvious fondness for *cordel* verse; he seems to delight in its imitation. Yet to view this process merely as some sort of nostalgic emulation or legitimation of a vanishing poetic form—a mythopoeic exercise in its own right—implies the absence of all ironic distance and comical exaggeration on the novelist's part, thus missing the point of his satirical intent.

A more accurate appraisal of Amado's *cordel* borrowings in *Tereza Batista* would probably concede his cultivation of both parody and stylization. Besides the comically grotesque section titles and xylographs

and the heroine's superlative nature, parodic elements in the novel include such things as the ABC form of the middle section, the supernatural with its attendant theurgic occurrences, and perhaps even the
work's prevailing hyperbolic cast. In each of these cases, the novelist
seems to be deliberately overstating some of the excesses of the *folheto,*
not to ridicule this naive poetry, to be sure, but in order to focus the
reader's attention on its esthetic incongruities in a gentle, ironic manner—in a word, to demystify them. As he tends to do also with many
of the characters of his mature novels, Amado distances himself from
the conventions of *cordel* literature just enough to be able to poke fun
at them, but not enough to totally deprive them of his indulgence and
authorial sympathy.

That he does indeed focus considerable irony on the formal trappings
of the very popular literature that he imitates—if not also upon himself
as an imitator—is made manifestly clear with the intervention of secondary narrator Cuíca de Santo Amaro, the late Bahian *cordel* poet,
towards the middle of the novel's penultimate section (*Tereza,*
301–4).[14] Although not technically a part of the parody, the intrusion
serves to comically underscore many of the eccentricities associated
with the *folheto* and its grassroots practitioners. Cuíca, while all the
while maintaining an adulatory attitude toward his interlocutor (the
novel's main narrator), decries the habit of many of his fellow *trovadores*
(popular poets) of sensationalizing or deliberately altering the facts of
an incident merely to sell more copies of their leaflets. He notes the
occurrence of this phenomenon even in some cover woodcuts. He also
makes mention of the presence in some *cordel* poems of what he considers to be forced rhyme and deficient metrical patterns. At the same
time, he often seems to be unaware of his own logical and moral inconsistencies, lamenting the fact that the main narrator is not a politician since the latter are wont to spend their constituents' money in
order to insure that they receive a "good press" from popular poets such
as himself. Despite his apparent venality, though, he is quick to claim
total truthfulness in his works and seems unable to comprehend why
he was jailed, threatened, and forced to destroy his leaflets by lawyers
representing the late Dr. Emiliano's family, whose transgressions he
had mercilessly aired in an obscene poem chronicling the late industrialist's scandalous demise.[15]

It is this pornographic element of *cordel* that receives the greatest
attention from the popular poet, who in real life was known for his
frequent cultivation of ithyphallic verse.[16] After quoting a scabrous

rhyme that circulated in the wake of Emiliano's death, he comments with obvious delight on a few of the best known *folhetos* on the topic, including his own. Each of them has a title that is as ludicrous as it is salacious: *The Old Man Who Died Humping a Virgin, The Death of the Master atop the Maid, The Last Screw of the Doctor Who Died at the Moment of Truth,* and so forth. Ribaldry is exploited to the utmost. Facts are exaggerated or even ignored. Cuíca observes that one of the poems is the filthiest that he has ever read. Another, he states, though containing few four-letter words, is so sexually explicit that it makes a man want to sleep with the first woman he sees. And the death scene is so moving that, after reading it, one longs to die in the same pleasant way. Others, despite their provocative titles, are, in Cuíca's opinion, unworthy of reading, for they have no prurient value nor do they make the reader laugh.

Part of Amado's satirical criticism here is obviously shared by the secondary narrator. Cuíca, though he is at times mildly amused by some of his competitors' most outlandish embellishments and is not above engaging in the practice himself, objects vociferously to their distorting the facts beyond all recognition for personal gain. One need not consign the late doctor's soul to hell or depict Tereza as having gone mad and killed herself, he claims, to write a good *cordel* poem. Much of the author's satire, however, remains inaccessible to him. Some of it seems, indeed, to be directed toward him inasmuch as he reflects, in the novelist's opinion, the values and tastes of the typical *folheto* poet. Thus, along with Amado, we laugh *at* him, not *with* him, when he advances the preposterous notion that a chapbook (or work of literature, in general) must either exhilarate or titillate the reader in order to be considered worthwhile. As is the case, too, with some of his other esthetic preferences and with his seeming unawareness of his own moral contradictions, Cuíca thus becomes the unwitting butt of the author's satire, a good example of what Freud referred to as "naive humor."[17]

Thus, despite the fact that it is not part of the parody proper, Cuíca's narration serves to reinforce the author's burlesquing of the conventions of *literatura de cordel* and perhaps ultimately to satirize, to lay bare, some of Amado's own esthetic techniques and precepts, particularly those that he appears to borrow from or at least have in common with Brazilian popular poetry. The mention of ludicrous titles, rhymes, and woodcuts of the kind associated with many *folhetos* echoes the author's apparent parodic intentions in the novel in progress. Cuíca may or may

not share in the joke, but Amado clearly sets up an ironic distance
between himself and these elements. The *trovador*'s pronouncements on
such matters as pornography, narrative veracity versus hyperbole, and
the proper functions of literature seem to go a step further. Not only
do they constitute a metafictional supplement to the parody in progress, but they also possess a decidedly self-reflexive character for both
novel and novelist alike.

There is yet another, more subtle effect of parody in *Tereza Batista*.
It has to do not so much with the author's satirizing the imitated genre
or his own novelistic techniques as it does with our reading and natu-
ralizing the text at hand. By clothing the latter in the traditional garb
of naive popular poetry, Amado, I believe, is seeking to exempt the
narrative from some of the usual generic assumptions that are made in
novel reading. For example, we are invited by the presence of the caricatural woodcuts and by the hyperbolic section titles to go a degree or
two further than normal in the willing suspension of skepticism with
which we approach a fictional text. What would have surely seemed
out of place and thoroughly unconvincing in the empirically oriented
novel—wooden, larger-than-life characters, magical solutions, and
meddling divinities—strikes us as being entirely verisimilar within the
guidelines of *cordel* literature, and thus we are willing to accept these
elements as part of the author's parody, partial though it may be. Much
the same thing can be said of the lack of suspense occasioned by the
informativeness of the section titles themselves; we are asked to view
it not as a novelistic defect but as a generic peculiarity of the formulaic
literature parodied.

Other *folheto* borrowings might indeed be better classified as "stylistic" rather than parodic. Chief among these are several of the novel's
plot motifs that appear to be of *cordel* or earlier folkloric origin. Part of
the literary worth of *Tereza Batista* resides precisely in the author's having woven a number of such popular plot motifs into its story line.
Another part, though, rests with the manner in which this appropriation occurred, with whether the novelist simply repeated the narrative
formula without transforming it or instead subjected it to some twist
or other ironic narrative modification that might serve to call attention
to its artificiality. Both processes seem to have occurred, although it is
not always entirely clear just which of the two is present in a given
case.

Certainly, there is something of parody itself in Amado's choice of a
prostitute to incarnate the time-honored role of the "warrior maiden,"

an irreverent reversal of what is itself a previous irreverent reversal. A similar irony may be seen in the application of several of the other traditional stereotypes and plot motifs to Tereza's adventures. We have previously noted this phenomenon in the episodes of the smallpox epidemic and the strike. On the other hand, there would seem to be little more than stylization in the novelist's appropriation of the popular plot motif of the wicked *fazendeiro* (plantation owner) who sexually enslaves virgins, a motif Curran identifies as being common to the *cordel* tradition. [18] The same might be said of both the episode of the usurer's punishment and the love story of Tereza Batista and Januário Gereba. The first of these is firmly rooted in the cycle of morality narratives and in the numerous stories of trickery that run throughout *folheto* poetry. The second, despite the obvious irony of the heroine's prostitute status, differs little from the countless "love-conquers-all" tales traditional in literature the world over. Whatever their basic nature, though—parodic or "stylistic"—all such borrowings serve to emphasize the essentially literary or art-imitating (as opposed to mimetic or reality-imitating) orientation of the text in question.

As regards the narrative's counterclaim, that of being a factual account of actual persons and events—a reflection of reality rather than art—there is likewise much in the text to substantiate this assertion. We have already listed above a few of the prefatory devices that the author uses to affirm the heroine's veracity. Curran appears to regard the presence of both the principal narrator and the various secondary narrators of *Tereza Batista* as reminiscent of the popular narrator of the *literatura de cordel*. [19] While there is something to be said for this view— several such narrators do indeed recall the orality and arrogations of total accuracy found in many Brazilian chapbooks—they would appear to have no clear counterparts in actual *folheto* poetry and thus do not seem to be part of the parody per se. Earlier, we noted the authenticating function exercised by the authorial narrator insofar as he is seen as representing the novelist. Much the same thing could be said of the secondary narrators, particularly those who are identified as real persons, such as Camafeu de Oxóssi, Mãe Senhora, Cuíca de Santo Amaro, and Eulália Leal Amado, the author's late mother. [20] Their accounts of the various exploits of the fictional heroine ironically serve to document her "real-life" existence. So, too, do the references made by several of them to other *folhetos* that purportedly deal as well with her adventures. What is more, the fact that each narrator knows only one aspect of Tereza's story (none appears to know all of it) provides the otherwise static, unidimensional heroine with the illusion (but only the illusion) of "roundness." A similar role is played by the occasional novelistic interior monologues. Narrative distance is relinquished, and an omniscient voice is allowed to reveal Tereza's (and others') thoughts and feelings, her various motivations, as if the novelist in Amado felt the need to compensate for the inherent narrative limitations of the would-be *cordel* poet. Both of these devices—the dramatized narrators and the interior monologues—tend to detract from the illusion that the work is indeed a *folheto* in prose.

In the end, Tereza Batista is probably more the result of art mirroring art than she is the reflection of the empirical world. Her verisimilitude is more generic—or parodic—than mimetic. Despite the principal narrator's claims of her historicity, claims supported by the testimony of the various, often flesh-and-blood secondary narrators, she remains a predictable yet at the same time opaque and eminently unconvincing figure as the heroine of a novel. She is definitely meant to cohere at some other level of verisimilitude, and only by heeding the author's signposts and reading the book as a kind of *cordel* poem in prose can the text be satisfactorily naturalized and its protagonist fully appreciated.

Chapter Seven
Amado—Man of Letters or Literary Hack?

In the preceding chapters we have seen how Amado's fiction has changed over the last half century. The early novels and novelettes were marked by social consciousness and often by strong political commitment. At first they sought to document and denounce societal injustices at the expense of "literary" concerns. Characters were usually of a single piece; virtue and vice were meted out according to a character's class affiliations. Protagonists were styled as proletarian heroes who rebelled against their ruling-class oppressors. Strikes and other popular uprisings were a fixture. As the author matured, greater emphasis was given to esthetics. Popular culture and Afro-Bahian religious ritual were deftly woven into the novelistic text. Amado became known not only for the crudity of his scenes and dialogues but also for the lyricism of his prose. Political sermonizing gave way to greater detachment. Caricature replaced invective. Characters, both poor and rich, were shown to be victims of economic and historical forces beyond their control. Still, many of the author's initial concerns and characteristics remained, while a number of his earlier excesses continued to predominate from time to time.

Some saw in *Gabriela, cravo e canela,* published in 1958, the appearance of a new Amado, divorced from Marxist ideology and dedicated to the cultivation of picaresque humor. According to this view, the novelist had turned his back on socialist realism altogether, replacing it with a commitment either to greater objectivity or to hedonism and bourgeois values. The particular assessment depended upon the critic's political leanings. Others, while conceding the transformation of Amado's "style," were not as convinced of his ideological conversion. They acknowledged that the novelist seemed to have veered away from prescriptive socialist realism, but regarded *Gabriela* more as a switch of tactics than as a wholesale retreat from a leftist worldview. Whatever their opinions of the change, however, most scholars were in agreement that *Gabriela* constituted a watershed in the author's literary develop-

ment. With the publication of each subsequent work this view gained
increased validity. There was, to be sure, no shortage of social criticism
in these novels, but much of it could best be described as satire rather
than polemic. Nor was there a dearth of lyricism, coarseness, violence,
caricature, folk culture, or Afro-Bahian religious ritual. If anything,
there was an intensification of such elements. Yet virtually everything
was suffused with humor and irony, to the point that it was sometimes
difficult to tell just where the author's sympathies lay.

But if humor was the key to this new phase, it was not exclusive to
it. Caricature had long been one of the primary supports of Amadian
fiction. So, too, had other forms of comical overstatement, as well as
such occasional phenomena as sarcasm, class humor, playful anecdotes,
and ribaldry. What was new was the proliferation of such techniques.
To the comical overstatement of the earlier works was added ironic
understatement. This was evident both in the author's greater use of
verbal irony and in the increased incidence of incongruous juxtaposi-
tions. Among the other humorous and ironic devices that became hallmarks of the "new" Amado were wit, parody, pastiche, double
perspective, the ironic narrator, the introduction of roman à clef characters, and the intervention of the supernatural. We have discussed
most of these as they appear in one or more of the author's later works.

In the course of this study, we have seen how the novelist's increased
use of irony, wit, and incongruous juxtaposition, besides lending
greater playfulness and irreverence to his fiction, has served to call into
question the dogmatism of political ideologies and religions. In particular, the various forms of irony have contributed to a relativization
of novelistic truth as Amado has gone from a classbound, black-or-
white mode of characterization to one dominated by various shades of
gray. In *Quincas* and *Comandante* we noted the importance of double
perspective in the creation of such a climate of uncertainty. In *Tereza
Batista* we examined the author's use of multiple, unreliable narrators
to achieve a similar effect. To the degree that such devices have become
a common feature of Amado's novels, the latter may be seen as having
replaced an essentially monologic narrative discourse with greater
dialogism.

Like irony, incongruous juxtaposition, and double perspective, the
introduction of real-life characters and the intercession of Afro-Bahian
divinities in *Dona Flor* and the later novels have, as we have noted,
served to variegate the fictional universe. Through a series of clever
displacements, characters à clef have themselves been juxtaposed in-

congruously with fictional personages, thus producing a kind of homogenization of fact and fantasy in which the boundaries of each are playfully expunged. Much the same thing can be said of the mischievous Yoruban gods. Their very presence in Amado's later novels, alongside fictional and real-life figures, has resulted in an expansion of the narrow confines of the empirical world, which several critics have identified with magic realism. By their roguishness, they are drawn ever more closely to the picaresque antiheroes that Amado is wont to portray. Furthermore, insofar as they intervene in human affairs in the manner of dei ex machina, the author's supernatural characters, whose existence he regards as metaphorical, perform a wish-fulfillment function, ironically reaffirming the necessity for the dispossessed themselves to redress social abuses, given the unlikelihood of religious or political solutions.

We have also analyzed the role of parody or pastiche in *Gabriela* (the chronicle), *Quincas* (the Gospels), *Tereza Batista* (*literatura de cordel*), and, to a lesser extent, *Dona Flor* (recipes and menus). From our findings, it would seem that Amado has used both parody proper and stylization of other genres and works in the novels treated. It appears, moreover, that his purposes in so doing have not always been the same, but have varied from book to book. To the extent that he has maintained a certain critical distance, Amado has engaged in parody as a means of satirizing a particular genre, such as the Renaissance *crônica* or the contemporary *literatura de cordel*. Besides mocking some of the most visible characteristics of these genres, he has sometimes used the technique to effect irreverent twists on the plot formulas traditionally associated with them. The stylistic appropriation of the camp trappings of these literary forms has also allowed him to claim exemption from some of the criteria we use in reading novels, despite the fact that his identification with the appropriated genres is only partial. There is likewise often an ironic dimension to such imitation insofar as the novel's everyday characters and actions may be seen to contrast markedly with the lofty, mock-heroic or mock-exotic trappings appropriated.

We have also witnessed the occasional metafictional and self-deprecatory roles of parody in *Tereza Batista*. In *Quincas,* however, the author's use of ironic pastiche appears to be aimed not so much at the Gospels or the events therein recounted, although it does indeed have the effect of questioning religious dogmatism. *Quincas* is rather primarily a prefigurative tale that makes use of a submerged Passion symbolism as a means of irreverently satirizing contemporary class *ethoi*.

And in *Dona Flor,* the menus and culinary formulas seem to function more as class indicators and enhancers of the overall sensuality of the narrative than as a vehicle for the lampooning of cookbooks.

In recent years, Amado has increasingly become the target of criticism of younger Brazilian and non-Brazilian literary scholars. The principal allegations involve such things as populism and the consequent romanticization of poverty, sexual and racial stereotyping, inordinate prolixity and repetition of episodes and characters, pandering to the values of the marketplace, and failure to break away from timeworn nineteenth-century narrative models. Far from superseding earlier criticisms, such accusations have often been coupled with renewed charges of pornography and Manichean characterization, albeit from different quarters. Several of these assertions are borne out to one degree or another by the foregoing analysis. Others are not. A brief look at the issue is in order.

There is no denying the long-windedness of Amado's narrative style. Unamuno's well-known characterization of writers as being either oviparous or viviparous would undoubtedly include the Bahian novelist in the latter category. Part of his reputation as a storyteller has always been based on his reported habit of composing his novels on a typewriter without previous drafts and with little or no subsequent revision. Never at ease with the lean prose style of a Ramos or a Hemingway, Amado seems to have turned to parody of bygone and popular genres, starting with *Gabriela,* in a deliberate attempt to make a virtue of necessity. He appears indeed to have strengthened his traditional reliance on verbal excess in the process, at times fairly reveling in the discursiveness of his narrators as if to reaffirm his own affiliations with the Latin oratorical tradition. Nor is there any doubt that the author has frequently appropriated earlier episodes and characters for use in subsequent novels. He has openly admitted to having reprised several strike scenes, for instance, simply to see how his previous treatment of them would be altered by greater infusions of humor and farce.

Whether such practices should be regarded as defects, however, is another matter. In his monograph on João Guimarães Rosa, Jon Vincent has labeled the various features of the traditional regionalist novel present in *Sagarana* as "deceptive simplicities," which, he feels, tend to obscure the underlying complexities of the work.[1] Notwithstanding the differences between the fiction of Rosa and Amado, much the same thing can be said, I believe, of many of the latter's recent novels. The leisurely verbosity of the narrative style, the presence of chatty, bumbling narrators, the tongue-in-cheek imitation of older and popular literature, and even the author's recourse to superannuated literary models often belie the fundamental sophistication of the works. Critics take the wordiness and trite formulas at face value without penetrating their inherent double-voicedness. They see in Amado's imitation of naive genres the attempt at mystification, but fail to notice its concomitant demystifying thrust. The novelist's propensity to caricature and his neoromantic identification with the Brazilian masses are cited as proof of his literary naïveté. But his desacralization of canonical discourses and the perspicacity of his social satire escape detection.

This is not to say that all such criticisms are invalid, only that they have sometimes been shortsighted or overdone. As we noted above, several of the most frequent allegations seem to be at least partially substantiated by the preceding analysis. Such is the case of sexual and racial stereotyping. Despite the author's emphasis on women's emancipation in *Gabriela* and despite his portrayal of some strong female figures, such as Malvina and Ofenísia, the novel's protagonist is eminently stereotypical. Gabriela may not be the traditional passive female character. Nor can she be said to represent the only paradigm on which the novelist has fashioned his *mulata* figures. But perhaps more than any other female personage in modern Brazilian literature, she incarnates the quintessential exotic *mulata,* often held up as the sexual ideal of Brazilian males. Not that strong-willed or unstereotyped women characters are in short supply in Amado's fiction. Many are to be found as early as *Mar morto* and *Terras do sem fim.* But they are joined by a sizable number of golden-hearted prostitutes and *mulata* caricatures, who sometimes seem to be more a projection of the author's male ego than a reflection of the empirical world. Amado's record on female characterization is thus a checkered one.

The novelist's populism also leaves ample room for criticism. The increased use of irony for characterization since *Gabriela* may have mitigated a strict class-line distribution of virtue, endowing the text with greater pluralism and discursive relativity, but it has not eliminated the author's identification with the poor altogether. On the contrary, much of the irony employed is of the stable variety, in which the "author's meaning" is clearly discernible rather than concealed. *Quincas, Dona Flor,* and *Tereza Batista* confirm the novelist's partiality in this regard. On the other hand, to adduce what is clearly a sentimental and perhaps naive neoromantic populism as evidence of the novelist's justification of poverty, superstition, and underdevelopment strikes me as far-fetched and disingenuous, a highly suspect assertion at best.

There is likewise something to be said for the notion that Amado's later fiction persists in the "closed," authoritarian molds of the nineteenth-century novel, often leaving little for the reader to supply. Some recent articles have attributed this tendency, along with the novelist's insistence on sex and violence, to his catering to the values of the marketplace.[2] Implicit in them is the suggestion that by so doing he has compromised his literary integrity, preferring a quick profit over esthetic quality. While it is hoped that the foregoing analysis of selected aspects of Amado's recent fiction will serve to dispel some of the stereotyping of these works as potboilers, it seems to me that further examination of this topic, as it relates to Amado and others, is appropriate and might indeed yield valuable insights.

Such an in-depth inquiry is beyond the purview of the present study. Suffice it to say here that Amado's case is strikingly similar to those of several well-known Brazilian leftist playwrights who in recent years have forsaken the stage to write television soap operas.[3] There is no denying the fact that such mass-media productions are considerably more lucrative to the author. Yet their audience is also vastly larger, thus giving the writer greater potential to shape the opinions of a larger number of people, albeit within the inevitable ideological constraints imposed by the owners of the medium. There is no doubt that Amado, like these writers, must pay a price in order to have access to such a mass audience. There are compromises to be made, both stylistic and ideological. The question is just how far one can go without compromising basic principles. To what degree is the writer using the medium rather than being used by it?

Brazilian cultural critic and sociologist Roberto Da Matta has detected in *Dona Flor* and other latter-day Amadian novels a "triadic" structure, in which the attempt to conciliate polar opposites leads to a third, synthetic position, which itself assumes a positive value rather than being regarded as something "monstrous" or "grotesque."[4] In Da Matta's opinion, it is this triadic structure that most differentiates the novelist's later works from those published prior to 1958, which he considers to be dualistic and ultimately monologic. He goes on to associate this tendency toward reconciliation with such traditional Brazilian institutions as the *jeitinho* (finding a solution), moderation, and the concession of personal favors, which are themselves grounded on a "relational" or integrational ethic. Unlike Anglo-Americans, with their passion for conflict, dichotomy, and separation, Brazilians have historically hybridized everything from their religious beliefs to their racial configuration, he claims. And it is this basic precept that Amado has recognized by structuring his later novels so as to emphasize the relational element.

Compromise of tactics or of strategy and its underlying values? The question remains and is not likely to be settled any time soon. The novelist's devoted admirers will undoubtedly continue to deny the inevitable contradictions in his latter-day fiction, while his most vocal detractors will point to its flaws, but refuse to concede its esthetic qualities and sophistication. Meanwhile, Amadian literary critics will no doubt persist in their Sisyphean effort to dispel such stereotypes.

Notes and References

Chapter One

1. Zélia Gattai, *Um chapéu para viagem,* 3d ed. (Rio de Janeiro: Record, 1983), 153–56.
2. Ibid., 113.
3. "Carta a uma leitora sobre romance e personagens," in *Jorge Amado, povo e terra: 40 anos de literatura* (Saõ Paulo: Martins, 1972), 25.
4. "Discurso de posse na Academia Brasileira," in *Jorge Amado, povo e terra,* 13.
5. See Walnice Nogueira Galvão, "Amado: Respeitoso, respeitável," in *Saco de gatos: Ensaios críticos* (São Paulo: Duas Cidades, 1976), 16, 21; and Daphne Patai, "Jorge Amado: Morals and Marvels," in *Myth and Ideology in Contemporary Brazilian Fiction* (Rutherford, N.J.: Fairleigh Dickinson University Press, 1983), 130.

Chapter Two

1. Gilberto Freyre, *New World in the Tropics: The Culture of Modern Brazil* (New York: Vintage, 1963), 217.
2. Miécio Táti, "Estilo e revolução no romance de Jorge Amado," in *Jorge Amado, povo e terra,* 125–43.
3. Affonso Romano de Sant'Anna, *Análise estrutural de romances brasileiros,* 4th ed. (Petrópolis: Vozes, 1977), 43.
4. Roger Bastide, "Sobre o romancista Jorge Amado," in *Jorge Amado, povo e terra,* 46.
5. Antônio Cândido, "Poesia, documento e história," in *Brigada ligeira* (São Paulo: Martins, 1945); rpt. in *Jorge Amado, povo e terra,* 113, 115.
6. Adolfo Casais Monteiro, in *O diabo,* Lisbon, 1937; rpt. in *Jorge Amado: 30 anos de literatura* (São Paulo: Martins, 1961), 124.
7. Érico Veríssimo, "A grande aventura de Baldo," *O Jornal,* Rio de Janeiro, 1935; rpt. in *Jorge Amado: 30 anos de literatura,* 112.
8. Octávio Tarquínio de Souza, "Jubiabá," *Diário de notícias,* Rio de Janeiro, 1935; rpt. in *Jorge Amado: 30 anos de literatura,* 101.
9. Luís Costa Lima, in *A literatura no Brasil,* ed. Afrânio Coutinho, 2d ed., (Rio de Janeiro: Sul Americana, 1970), 5:310.
10. Cândido, "Poesia," 122.
11. Sérgio Milliet, as quoted in Miécio Táti, *Jorge Amado: Vida e obra* (Belo Horizonte: Itatiaia, 1961), 125.

12. Paulo Dantas, in *Diário popular,* São Paulo, 1943; excerpted in *Jorge Amado: 30 anos de literatura,* 209.

13. Cândido, "Poesia," 113.

14. Sant'Anna, *Análise,* 43.

15. See Nancy T. Baden, "Jorge Amado: Storyteller of Bahia (A Study of Narrative Technique)" (Ph.D. Diss., University of California, Los Angeles, 1971), 105–6.

16. Fred P. Ellison, *Brazil's New Novel: Four Northeastern Masters* (Berkeley and Los Angeles: University of California Press, 1954), 91.

17. Ibid., 89.

Chapter Three

1. It could be argued, of course, that such devices, particularly the lengthy titles, are equally reminiscent of other literary traditions, such as the medieval novels of chivalry, the popular ballad, or folk literature. See, for example, Doris J. Turner, "The Poor and Social Symbolism: An Examination of Three Novels of Jorge Amado," (Ph.D. Diss., St. Louis University, 1967), 60–61; and M. Cavalcanti Proença, "Senhora Gabriela, na cidade das letras," *Jornal do Brasil,* Rio de Janeiro, 1958; rpt. in *Jorge Amado: 30 anos de literatura,* 258. Amado clearly draws on some of these other sources in his use of similar devices in such later works as *Pastores, Tereza Batista,* and *Tieta.*

2. For further discussion of this distinction, see chapter 6.

3. Richard A. Mazzara, "Poetry and Progress in Jorge Amado's *Gabriela, cravo e canela,*" *Hispania* 46 (1963): 551–56.

4. Turner, "Poor," 56.

5. Juan M. Corominas, "La estructura femenina en la novela *Gabriela, cravo e canela,*" *Encruzilhadas/Crossroads* 2, Proceedings of the Second Symposium on Portuguese Traditions, 10–11 May 1979, ed. Claude L. Hulet (Los Angeles, 1982), 91–96; "Incidencia femenina en la estructura de *Gabriela, cravo e canela,*" *Hispania* 68 (1985): 484–89.

6. Ann Pescatello, "The *Brazileira:* Images and Realities in Writings of Machado de Assis and Jorge Amado," in *Female and Male in Latin America: Essays,* ed. Ann Pescatello (Pittsburgh: University of Pittsburgh Press, 1973), 29–58. For purposes of the comparison, Pescatello contrasts Amado's heroines with those of Joaquim Maria Machado de Assis (1839–1908).

7. According to the novelist ("Carta," 31), it is with Gabriela that women's liberation begins in the Bahian cacao region, as it is fictionalized in the present work.

8. In a monograph, *A mulher na sociedade de classes: Mito e realidade* (Petrópolis: Vozes, 1976), Heleieth Iara Bongiovani Saffioti notes that in the patriarchal society of colonial Brazil "it was normal for a fifteen-year-old woman to be married and have a child; many became mothers at the age of

thirteen. Raised in a strict patriarchal environment, such child-mothers, upon marriage, escaped the control of their fathers only to fall into their husbands' sphere of control. Foreign chroniclers tell of the cruelty with which both unmarried and married women were punished whenever there was the slightest suspicion that they had deceived the watchful eye of a father or husband to engage in alleged flirtations" (168).

9. A similar opinion is held by Carl N. Degler with respect to the prostitution of black and mulatto women in colonial Brazil (*Neither Black Nor White: Slavery and Race Relations in Brazil and the United States* [New York: Macmillan, 1971], 190); cf. Roger Bastide, "Dusky Venus, Black Apollo," *Race* 3 (November 1961): 11; and Saffioti, *Mulher*, 169: "It is obvious that the chastity of the great majority of women in the ruling classes was made possible only by the prostitution of other women."

10. For a discussion of women in medieval literature, see Joan M. Ferrante, *Woman as Image in Medieval Literature: From the Twelfth Century to Dante* (New York: Columbia University Press, 1975); see also Northrop Frye, *The Secular Scripture: A Study of the Structure of Romance* (Cambridge: Harvard University Press, 1976), chapter 3, for treatment of the role of female characters in romance.

11. The shrew, the disobedient wife, the adulteress, and the *filha maldita* (evil daughter) are but some of the familiar transgressive female characters in literature who regularly receive punishment for their "sins."

12. According to José Calazans ("A Ofenísia de Jorge Amado," *Jornal da Bahia* [Salvador, 1960], excerpted in *Jorge Amado: 30 anos de literatura*, 301), the legend of Ofenísia comes from Sergipe and is based upon a real-life figure who scandalized the patriarchal society of that state in the midnineteenth century with her celebrated amours.

13. Notes Simone de Beauvoir (*The Second Sex*, trans. and ed. H. M. Parshley [New York: Bantam, 1961], 177–78): "If the husband does not succeed in keeping his wife in the path of virtue, he shares in her fault; in the eyes of society his misfortune is a blot on his honor; there are civilizations severe enough to require him to kill the wrongdoer in order to dissociate himself from her crime."

14. Frye, *Secular Scripture*, 81ff., briefly treats the topic of woman as sacrificial victim in literature.

15. Mazzara, "Poetry," 554.

16. Amado seems to be genuinely proud of Malvina as a character. In "Carta," he admits to having "seen" her from time to time in a number of courageous, rebellious young women whom he has met in his travels over the years. He also confesses to imagining her as she might be today: "I don't know why, but I see her working perhaps as a doctor in a hospital, achieving something, accomplishing something great."

17. Pescatello, "Brazileira," 50.

18. Ironically, critic José Paulo Paes regards Gabriela as the most convincing of Amado's female characters ("*Gabriela, cravo e canela,*" in *Pequeno dicionário de literatura brasileira,* ed. José Paulo Paes and Massaud Moisés [São Paulo: Cultrix, 1969], 107). Miécio Táti, writing in 1960, expresses a similar view, noting that Gabriela is both realistic and highly individualized as a character (*Jorge Amado: Vida e obra,* 161, 164–65). According to Elizabeth Schlomann Lowe ("The 'New' Jorge Amado," *Luso-Brazilian Review* 6.2 [December 1969]: 78), "Amado masterfully portrays the psychology of Gabriela." In a review of the English translation of *Gabriela* ("The Town's Story Is the Land's," *New York Times Book Review,* 16 September 1962, 1), Juan De Onis contrasts Gabriela, whom he considers to be a "round," individualized character, with the "flat symbols" typical of the novelist's earlier fiction. For an opposing view, one that sees Gabriela more as a symbol, as I do, see Antônio Rangel Bandeira's article on *Gabriela* (*Última hora* [São Paulo, 1958], as excerpted in *Jorge Amado: 30 anos de literatura,* 284–85) and that of Fritz Teixeira Sales ("O chão de Gabriela," *Folha de Minas,* Belo Horizonte, 1958, as excerpted in *Jorge Amado: 30 anos de literatura,* 298–99).

19. States Malcolm N. Silverman ("Algumas observações sobre as personagens de Jorge Amado," *Moderna ficção brasileira: Ensaios,* trans. João Guilherme Linke [Rio: Civilização Brasileira; Brasília: Instituto Nacional do Livro, 1978], 151): "Attitudes change all around her, but she herself, unlike her partner Nacib, remains unchanged: her purity of soul, if not of body, needs no transition; she is from the outset ideal."

20. Curiously, the English translation does not contain the original section subtitle. Silverman (ibid., 151, n. 47) notes that Amado, in correspondence with him, has confirmed that Gabriela is indeed meant to personify the Brazilian people.

21. For a largely sympathetic view of Amado's populism, see Jon S. Vincent, "Jorge Amado: Politics and the Novel," (Ph.D. Diss., University of New Mexico, 1970), 409–11; see also Baden, "Jorge Amado: Storyteller," 127–28, 235. In *Brazil's New Novel* (103ff.), Ellison discusses the novelist's rather Manichean portrayal of characters along class lines in his early fiction. According to an unsigned review of *Tereza Batista* appearing in a prominent Brazilian news magazine ("Jorge, descansado de guerra," *Visão,* 15 January 1973, 70), Amado's populist creed tends to be acritical and thus to legitimize superstition, poverty and backwardness. Walnice Nogueira Galvão ("Amado: Respeitoso," 16) seems to hold a similar view.

Chapter Four

1. Whether by design or not, the Hegelian dialectic seems to be the organizing principle for several other Amadian works, including *Gabriela* and *Dona Flor.*

2. Lowe, "The 'New' Jorge Amado," 73–82.

3. Affonso Romano de Sant'Anna, "De como e porque Jorge Amado em *A morte e a morte de Quincas Berro D'água* é um autor carnavalizador, mesmo sem nunca se preocupado com isso," *Tempo brasileiro 74: Jorge Amado, Km 70* (July–September 1983): 57–58.

4. For a discussion of overdetermination, see Sigmund Freud, *The Interpretation of Dreams,* trans. and ed. James Strachey (New York: Avon, 1965), 318, 342.

5. All biblical quotations are taken from the Revised Standard Version.

6. The division of garments in both cases represents a symbolic *sparagmos,* or ritual tearing apart of the sacrificial body, a phenomenon treated by Northrop Frye in his *Anatomy of Criticism: Four Essays* (Princeton, N.J.: Princeton University Press, 1957), 148, 192–93, 222.

7. J. E. Cirlot, *A Dictionary of Symbols,* trans. Jack Sage (New York: Philosophical Library, 1962), 103; for a discussion of Janaína, or Iemanjá, see Amado's *Mar morto,* 28th ed. (São Paulo: Martins, 1970), 78ff.

8. Cirlot (*Dictionary,* 109) attributes this association in part to the frog's amphibiousness—its serving as a link between land and water; cf. Jean Chevalier, *Dictionnaire des symboles* (Paris: Laffont, 1969), 391–92: "In the West itself, the frog has been regarded as a symbol of resurrection by reason of its metamorphoses."

Chapter Five

1. The movie version of *Dona Flor,* produced by Luiz Carlos Barreto and directed by his son Bruno Barreto, appeared in 1976. It starred Sônia Braga and José Wilker. The novel was also adapted for Broadway several years later under the title *Saravá.*

2. The association of eating and sex is not a casual one. Discussing "the very profound analogy which people throughout the world seem to find between copulation and eating," Claude Lévi-Strauss notes that "in Yoruba 'to eat' and 'to marry' are expressed by a single verb the sense of which is 'to win, to acquire'" (*The Savage Mind* [Chicago: University of Chicago Press, 1966], 105). Indeed, for the Yorubas "marrying and eating are one and the same thing," he adds (131). Brazilian popular speech makes a similar connection. *Comer* is widely used as a vulgar substitute for *copular.* So too are the verb *papar,* which means "to eat," and *mastigar,* "to chew." In view of the strong Yoruban influence on such things as religion and language in certain parts of Brazil, it is not unlikely that *comer* in its sexual sense represents a loanshift borrowed from Yoruba.

3. General descriptions are provided of the various dishes that appear in the recipes, in view of the importance of some of the ingredients to the analogy. For more on Brazilian cuisine, see Margarette de Andrade, *Brazilian Cookery: Traditional and Modern* (Rutland, Vt.: Tuttle, 1965).

4. Are we to interpret this equation of female and food as a reiteration

of the timeworn relegation of woman to the status of sex object? I think not. It seems to me that in the case of Flor the idea is rather a reflection of her own particular personality, as it has been molded by the very restrictive and sexist societal norms that the novelist seeks to invalidate.

5. The importance of food and cooking to Flor's personality and to the story itself may be seen not only in the recipes and menus but also in the introductory letter, which the protagonist uses to relay a recipe to the author himself. With regard to the former, Jon S. Vincent ("Jorge Amado: Politics," 259) has noted the fundamental importance of both cooking and lovemaking to Flor's psychological makeup. Meanwhile, the heroine's letter purportedly directed to Amado possesses the additional function of "authenticating" her real-life existence, tending as it does to homogenize the empirical world of the Bahian novelist with the fictional world that he has created.

6. Paulo Tavares, *Criaturas de Jorge Amado.* 2d ed. (Rio de Janeiro: Record; Brasília: Instituto Nacional do Livro, 1985), "Quadro de referência," before pagination.

7. Tavares (*Criaturas*) lists as 316 the total number of characters in *Dona Flor.* My own tabulation, using appendix 1 of his work ("Relação onomástica, com indicações biográficas, das personalidades reais ou lendárias mencionadas," 445–93) reveals a total of more than 145 real characters in the novel, a far cry from the half dozen or so found in *Gabriela* or the handful who turn up in *Quincas* and *Pastores.* Fully 85–90 percent of the real-life characters who appear in Amado's works before the end of 1966 are in *Dona Flor.*

8. The most notable exception prior to *Dona Flor* occurs in *Capitães da areia,* where two real-life figures, Don'Aninha and Querido de Deus, play significant parts in the story. According to Tavares (*Criaturas,* 485, 452), the former (Eugênia Ana dos Santos) was a famous Bahian *mãe-de-santo* (*candomblé* priestess) deceased in 1938, and the latter (Samuel Francisco de Sousa Barreto), a fisherman and distinguished *capoeirista* (Afro-Brazilian martial-arts expert), who died in 1950. For further information on Querido de Deus, see Amado's *Bahia de Todos os Santos: Guia das ruas e dos mistérios da cidade do Salvador,* 14th ed. (São Paulo: Martins, 1967), 236–38.

9. The real-life models for these characters were the late Norma dos Guimarães Sampaio, José Mirabeau Sampaio, Gisela do Prado Valadares, Héctor Julio Páride Bernabó (also known as Carybé), Lita Costa Porto, and Thales de Araújo Porto, respectively. For further information on them, consult Tavares, *Criaturas,* 255, 485; 356, 359, 485; 133, 491; 58–59, 453; 199, 481; 321, 481.

10. "Sugar and Spice," review of *Dona Flor and Her Two Husbands, Time,* 5 September 1969, 89; reference is to the Harriet de Onís translation (New York: Knopf, 1969).

11. Bruce A. Morrissette (in Joseph T. Shipley, ed., *Dictionary of World Literature,* new rev. ed. [Totowa, N.J.: Littlefield, Adams, 1968], 257) de-

fines *livre à clef* as "a work in which actual persons figure under fictitious names." Sylvan Barnet, Morton Berman, and William Burto (*A Dictionary of Literary Terms* [Boston: Little, Brown, 1960], 61) state that the roman à clef "uses contemporary historical figures as its chief characters, but they are disguised with fictitious names." Neither of these definitions is satisfactory for our purpose; both place unnecessary limitations on the subgenre.

12. *The Random House Dictionary of the English Language,* 2d ed., unabridged (New York: Random House, 1987).

13. Russell G. Hamilton ("Afro-Brazilian Cults in the Novels of Jorge Amado," *Hispania* 50 [1967]: 250, 252, n. 36) has observed this in-group phenomenon in Amado's fiction, both with respect to the comprehension of particular *candomblé* rituals and the understanding of roman à clef humor.

14. José Mirabeau Sampaio is a leading Bahian physician, painter, and sculptor, and a retired educator and shoe merchant (Tavares, *Criaturas,* 485). Caetano Veloso belongs to the generation of popular musicians and composers who came to prominence in the 1960s. He was early identified with the movement known as Tropicalismo. Zélia Gattai, a *paulista* by birth, has been married to Jorge Amado since 1945. She is a recognized author and photographer.

15. Mirandão was inspired by the late Bahian veterinarian and public official, José Rodrigues de Miranda Filho (Tavares, *Criaturas,* 242–43, 476). Arigof was the nickname of the late Bahian gambler and bohemian, Isaías Carvalho (ibid., 30, 456). Giovanni Guimarães is the late Bahian doctor and journalist (ibid., 133, 467).

16. Jenner Augusto da Silveira is a well-known Bahian painter, a native son of Sergipe (ibid., 158, 487; Ricardo Noblat, "Os personagens vivos de Jorge Amado," *Manchete,* 3 March 1973, 47). Carlos de Góis Mascarenhas is a Bahian attorney and politician (Tavares, *Criaturas,* 59, 474–75). Antônio Melquíades Cardoso e Silva was a Bahian poet, painter, journalist, and public official (ibid., 26, 487); I had the opportunity to meet him at Amado's house in April of 1974 and to verify the accuracy of the caricature.

17. See note 14.

18. José Júlio de Calasans Neto, the renowned Bahian woodcut artist, painter, and sculptor, is noted for his joke-telling ability (ibid., 55, 56, 454). José Vitalino de Barros Martins is the former owner of the now-defunct Livraria Martins Editora of São Paulo, which was Amado's publisher from 1941 to 1975 (ibid., 474).

19. Tibúrcio Alves Barreiros Filho is identified by Tavares (ibid., 329, 452) as a Bahian magistrate.

20. Noblat, "Personagens," 45.

21. Mário da Silva Cravo Júnior is a famous Bahian sculptor and painter (Tavares, *Criaturas,* 231, 460). Luís da Câmara Cascudo is the late Brazilian folklorist from Natal, Rio Grande do Norte (ibid., 456).

22. Gilberto Gil, like Veloso, became famous as a young poet and musician in the 1960s. He too espoused Tropicalismo.

23. Waldeloir Rego is a Bahian folklorist and jewelry designer (Tavares, *Criaturas,* 339–40, 482). Tavares (ibid., 490) identifies Dr. Epaminondas dos Santos Torres as the late Bahian engineer, intellectual, and city father.

24. Ibid., 480.

25. Marilda Alves Ramosandrade is, according to Tavares (ibid., 229, 448), a Brazilian motion-picture actress.

26. See note 15. Jaci and Ludmila Guimarães are discussed by Tavares (ibid., 154, 204, 467).

27. Dates of birth and death are taken from Tavares's *Criaturas.* It is Tavares also who indicates the period in which the story is supposed to have taken place ("Quadro de referência," before pagination).

28. Ibid., 457.

29. Ibid., 58–59, 141, 455.

30. See note 14. Tavares (ibid., 359) also identifies José Mirabeau Sampaio as the model for Zequito Mirabeau. See also Noblat, "Personagens," 45.

31. Floriano Teixeira is the famed artist and caricaturist who illustrated the Brazilian edition of *Dona Flor.* He appears with his real name in *Tereza* (457). Fernando Coelho, the Bahian artist, is discussed, along with several others of Amado's artist friends, by Antônio Celestino, *Gente da terra* (São Paulo: Martins, 1972), 127–32. He appears in his own right as a character in *Tereza* (457).

32. With respect to the process of association, Amado has noted, "In general, a character is a composite of several figures, combining the traits of various persons with whom I have come into contact. Now, even if you start out with a single figure, assuming that he is extraordinarily rich [as a character], as soon as you remove him from real life and place him in a novel alongside other figures and have him undergo conflicts extraneous to his normal life, he is changed and becomes another person" (Noblat, "Personagens," 44).

33. For further discussion of Manuel Querino and his works, see E. Bradford Burns, "Manuel Querino's Interpretation of the African Contribution to Brazil," *The Journal of Negro History* 59.1 (January 1974); 78–86. Martiniano do Bonfim is mentioned by Amado in *Bahia de Todos os Santos* (178) as having been one of the last Bahian *babalaôs* (Afro-Brazilian soothsayers). Miguel Arcanjo Barradas Santiago de Santana is treated by Noblat ("Personagens," 46). He also appears in *Tenda* (85) under his own name and is one of the secondary narrators in *Tereza* (243–45). See Tavares, *Criaturas,* 240, 485.

34. Information and quote taken from a personal interview with Amado at his home in Salvador, Bahia, on 30 November 1973.

35. Tavares, *Criaturas,* 81–82, 463.

36. *Bahia de Todos os Santos,* 252.

37. In fact, José Mirabeau Sampaio, in an interview with me (21 April

1974), confirmed that he is the only one of the group to have ever lived on that street.

38. This was corroborated by Amado in a 22 April 1974 interview with me.

39. One might detect a similar effect in the fictionalized history presented in many historical novels. For treatment of the "mimetic" and "historical" literary modes, consult Robert Scholes and Robert Kellogg, *The Nature of Narrative* (London: Oxford University Press, 1966), 13ff.

40. Wilson Martins, "A comédia baiana," in *Jorge Amado, povo e terra*, 174.

41. Malcolm Silverman ("An Examination of the Characters in Jorge Amado's *Ciclo da comédia baiana*," [Ph.D. Diss., University of Illinois, Urbana-Champaign, 1971], 298) relates the case of a noted Bahian clairvoyant, Madame Beatriz, who almost took Amado to court over his use of that name in *Pastores* for a loose-living mystic quack. In a 1960 article published in the *New York Times* (rpt. in *Jorge Amado: 30 anos de literatura*, 304–5), Antônio Callado tells how Jorge Medauar was attacked and almost killed in Ilhéus after writing a magazine story in which he identified a respectable local couple as having been Amado's model for Gabriela and Nacib in *Gabriela, cravo e canela*.

42. See "Carta," 3–36.

43. Harold Courlander, *Tales of the Yoruba Gods and Heroes* (Greenwich, Conn.: Fawcett, 1974), 23.

44. Joseph Campbell, *The Hero with a Thousand Faces*, Bollingen Series 17, 2d ed. (Princeton, N.J.: Princeton University Press, 1968), 19.

45. Afrânio Coutinho, "Do barroco ao rococó," in *A literatura no Brasil*, ed. Afrânio Coutinho, 2d ed., vol. 1 (Rio de Janeiro: Sul Americana, 1968), 144; Juarez da Gama Batista, *O barroco e o maravilhoso no romance de Jorge Amado*, (João Pessoa: Tipografia Chaves, 1973), 12ff.

Chapter Six

1. Reference here is to Menininha do Gantois, noted Bahian *mãe-de-santo*, who died in 1986. Tavares (*Criaturas*, 237, 477) lists her real name as Maria Escolástica da Conceição.

2. Caymmi, a Bahian born in 1914, has for many years been a popular Brazilian songwriter and performer. He is mentioned briefly in *Comandante* (227, 229) and is portrayed in *Dona Flor* as a struggling young musician who accompanies Vadinho and friends in a serenade of the heroine (116–19). See chapter 5, note 28.

3. Real figures serving as secondary narrators include Camafeu de Oxóssi (*Tereza*, 42–44), a Bahian entrepreneur and restaurateur (born 1915), whose real name is Ápio Patrocínio da Conceição; the late Miguel Santana

Obá Aré, a local *candomblé* official (*Tereza*, 243–45); Cuíca de Santo Amaro
(*Tereza*, 301–4), the late *cordel* poet (1919–65), born José Gomes; Mãe Senhora
(*Tereza*, 345–47); and Dona Lalu, the author's late mother (*Tereza*, 454–55)
(both mentioned earlier). Some of these characters appeared in Amado's earlier
novels. In addition, Brazilian romantic poet Antônio Castro Alves (1847–71)
serves as a narrator introducing one of the episodes (*Tereza*, 368–69). For
further information, see Tavares, *Criaturas*.

4. Walnice Nogueira Galvão ("Amado: Respeitoso," 18–19) decries
what she regards as the novelist's minute description of Capitão Justo's sadistic
sexual aberrations for the purpose of erotic titillation, charging that Amado
displays a certain admiration for the captain's amatory prowess. By contrast,
Paulo Tavares (*O baiano Jorge Amado e sua obra* [Rio de Janeiro: Record, 1980],
185) contends that Amado's Capitão Justo is essentially a symbol, "not strictly
a character in the same sense as the rest of his extensive gallery, but rather the
archetype of evil, the liberticide, the enemy of the people, the anti-human."

5. Mark Curran, *Jorge Amado e a literatura de cordel* (Salvador: Fundação
Cultural do Estado da Bahia, 1981), 62.

6. Calasans Neto also appears briefly as a character in *Tereza Batista*
(457). See chapter 5, note 18.

7. Candace Slater, "The Donzela Guerreira in a Brazilian *Folheto*,"
Encruzilhadas/Crossroads 2, Proceedings of the Second Symposium on Portuguese Traditions, 10–11 May 1979, ed. Claude L. Hulet (Los Angeles, 1982),
77–87. See also Candace Slater, *Stories on a String: The Brazilian* Literatura de
Cordel (Berkeley and Los Angeles: University of California Press, 1982),
152–53.

8. Curran, *Cordel*, 59.

9. Patai, *Myth*, 118.

10. Slater, *Stories on a String*, 14–15; Curran, *Cordel*, 65–66.

11. Frye, *Anatomy*, 33.

12. Patai, *Myth*, 114. The critic goes on to take Amado to task for what
she seems to regard as his attempt to pass off an expensive five hundred-page
novel as a work of Brazilian folklore (118).

13. Mikhail Mikhailovich Bakhtin, *The Dialogic Imagination: Four Essays*, ed. Michael Holquist; trans. Caryl Emerson and Michael Holquist
(Austin: University of Texas Press, 1981), 362–64; Yuri Tynianov, as quoted
in Tzvetan Todorov, *The Poetics of Prose*, trans. Richard Howard (Ithaca: Cor-
nell University Press, 1977), 245.

14. See note 3.

15. Ironically, Cuíca, like the novel's authorial narrator, does not confine
his account to the scurrilous details of Emiliano's death, as others have done,
but uses the event as an excuse to expose the corruption and decadence of the
late industrialist's family.

16. Cuíca's penchant for ribald verse is mentioned by Orígenes Lessa in

his book *Getúlio Vargas na literatura de cordel* (Rio de Janeiro: Documentário, 1973), 33; see also Curran, *Cordel,* 78.

17. "Naive humor," according to Freud, occurs when what normally would be considered witty or obscene is uttered by a child or uneducated adult who "has tried in good faith to draw a serious conclusion on the basis of his uncorrected ignorance" (Sigmund Freud, *Jokes and Their Relation to the Unconscious,* trans. James Strachey [New York: W. W. Norton, 1963], 183).

18. Curran, *Cordel,* 64.

19. Ibid., 54–55.

20. See note 3.

Chapter Seven

1. Jon Vincent, *João Guimarães Rosa,* Twayne World Authors Series 506 (Boston: Twayne, 1978), 17.

2. See Silviano Santiago ("O teorema de Walnice e a sua recíproca," in *Vale quanto pesa* [Rio de Janeiro: Paz e Terra, 1982], 69–88).

3. The most notable playwright to have done so is Alfredo Dias Gomes, a self-proclaimed Marxist, who has asserted that television has now become the theater of the masses.

4. Roberto Da Matta, "*Dona Flor e seus dois maridos:* Um romance relacional," *Tempo Brasileiro* 74: 3–33.

Selected Bibliography

PRIMARY WORKS

ABC de Castro Alves. São Paulo: Martins, 1941.

O amor de Castro Alves. Rio de Janeiro: Editora do Povo, 1947. (Later called *O amor do soldado.*)

Bahia boa terra Bahia. With Carybé and Flávio Damm. Rio de Janeiro: Image, 1967.

Bahia de Todos os Santos: Guia das ruas e dos mistérios da cidade do Salvador. São Paulo: Martins, 1945.

Brandão entre o mar e o amor. With Aníbal Machado, Graciliano Ramos, José Lins do Rego, and Rachel de Queiroz. São Paulo: Martins, 1942.

Cacau. Rio de Janeiro: Ariel, 1933.

Capitães da areia. Rio de Janeiro: José Olympio, 1937. *Captains of the Sands.* Translated by Gregory Rabassa. New York: Avon, 1988.

"De como o mulato Porciúncula descarregou o seu defunto." *Histórias da Bahia.* Rio de Janeiro: GRD, 1963.

Dona Flor e seus dois maridos: História moral e de amor. São Paulo: Martins, 1966. *Dona Flor and Her Two Husbands.* Translated by Harriet de Onís. New York: Knopf, 1969.

A estrada do mar. Estância, Sergipe: Tipografia Popular, 1938.

Farda, fardão, camisola de dormir: Fábula para acender uma esperança. Rio de Janeiro: Record, 1979. *Pen, Sword, Camisole: A Fable to Kindle a Hope.* Boston: Godine, 1985.

Gabriela, cravo e canela: Crônica de uma cidade do interior. São Paulo: Martins, 1958. *Gabriela, Clove and Cinnamon.* Translated by James L. Taylor and William Grossman. New York: Knopf, 1962.

O gato malhado e a andorinha sinhá: Uma história de amor. Rio de Janeiro: Record, 1976. *The Swallow and the Tom Cat.* Translated by Barbara Shelby Merello. New York: Delacorte, 1982.

"História do carnaval." *Antologia do carnaval.* Rio de Janeiro: O Cruzeiro, 1945.

Jubiabá. Rio de Janeiro: José Olympio, 1935. *Jubiabá.* Translated by Margaret Neves. New York: Avon, 1984.

Lenita. With Dias da Costa and Édison Carneiro. Rio de Janeiro: Coelho Branco Filho, 1930. (Serialized in 1929.)

Mar morto. Rio de Janeiro: José Olympio, 1936. *Sea of Death.* Translated by Gregory Rabassa. New York: Avon, 1984.

O menino grapiúna. Rio de Janeiro: Record, 1981.

O mistério dos MMM. With Viriato Correia, Dinah Silveira de Queiroz, Lúcio Cardoso, Herberto Salles, José Condé, João Guimarães Rosa, Antônio Callado, Orígenes Lessa, and Rachel de Queiroz. Rio de Janeiro: O Cruzeiro, 1962.

A morte e a morte de Quincas Berro D'água. Senhor 1 (June 1959): 50–66. (Published in 1961 in *Os velhos marinheiros;* later published as a separate volume.) *The Two Deaths of Quincas Wateryell.* Translated by Barbara Shelby. New York: Knopf, 1965.

"As mortes e o triunfo de Rosalinda." *Os dez mandamentos.* Rio de Janeiro: Civilização Brasileira, 1965.

O mundo da paz. Rio de Janeiro: Vitória, 1950.

O país do carnaval. Rio de Janeiro: Schmidt, 1931.

Os pastores da noite. São Paulo: Martins, 1964. *Shepherds of the Night.* Translated by Harriet de Onís. New York: Knopf, 1967.

São Jorge dos Ilhéus. São Paulo: Martins, 1944.

Seara vermelha. São Paulo: Martins, 1946.

Os subterrâneos da liberdade. São Paulo: Martins, 1954. *Os ásperos tempos, A agonia da noite, A luz no túnel.*

O sumiço da santa: Uma história de feitiçaria. Rio de Janeiro: Record, 1988.

Suor. Rio de Janeiro: Ariel, 1934.

Tenda dos milagres. São Paulo: Martins, 1969. *Tent of Miracles.* Translated by Barbara Shelby. New York: Knopf, 1971.

Tereza Batista cansada de guerra. São Paulo: Martins, 1972. *Tereza Batista: Home from the Wars.* Translated by Barbara Shelby. New York: Knopf, 1975.

Terra grapiúna. With Adonias Filho. Rio de Janeiro: Tempo Brasileiro, 1965.

Terras do sem fim. São Paulo: Martins, 1943. *The Violent Land.* Translated by Samuel Putnam. New York: Knopf, 1945.

Tieta do Agreste: Pastora de cabras ou a volta da filha pródiga, melodramático folhetim em cinco sensacionais episódios e comovente epílogo: Emoção e suspense! Rio de Janeiro: Record, 1977. *Tieta the Goat Girl; or, The Return of the Prodigal Daughter, a Melodramatic Serial Novel in Five Sensational Episodes, with a Touching Epilogue: Thrills and Suspense.* Translated by Barbara Shelby Merello. New York: Knopf, 1979.

Tocaia Grande: A face obscura. Rio de Janeiro: Record, 1984. *Showdown.* Translated by Gregory Rabassa. New York: Bantam, 1988.

Os velhos marinheiros: Duas histórias do cais da Bahia. São Paulo: Martins, 1961. (*A morte e a morte de Quincas Berro D'água* and *A completa verdade sobre as discutidas aventuras do Comandante Vasco Moscoso de Aragão, capitão de longo curso;* the latter was subsequently published separately as *Os velhos marinheiros ou o capitão de longo curso.*) *Home Is the Sailor.* Translated by Harriet de Onís. New York: Knopf, 1964.

Vida de Luiz Carlos Prestes, el caballero de la esperanza. Buenos Aires: Claridad,

1942. (First published in Brazil as *O cavaleiro da esperança* [São Paulo: Martins, 1945].)

SECONDARY WORKS

Books and Parts of Books

[Aguiar] Filho, Adonias. "Romance de testemunho." In *Modernos ficcionistas brasileiros*. 2d ser., 11–18. Rio de Janeiro: Tempo Brasileiro, 1965; rpt. in *Jorge Amado, povo e terra: 40 anos de literatura*, 195–202. São Paulo: Martins, 1972. Views Amado's novels as documentaries of urban and rural Bahia.

Almeida, Alfredo Wagner Berno de. *Jorge Amado: Política e literatura: Um estudo sobre a trajetória intelectual de Jorge Amado*. Rio de Janeiro: Campus, 1979. A discourse on the politics of Amado's fiction through *Gabriela*. Makes abundant reference to the published criticism, from which he extracts numerous citations. Includes a bibliography of primary and secondary sources, which, though not complete, contains many items not listed elsewhere.

Batista, Juarez da Gama. *O barroco e o maravilhoso no romance de Jorge Amado*. João Pessoa: Tipografia Chaves, 1973. Prizewinning essay that considers such elements as the novelist's reliance on the Afro-Brazilian supernatural, his use of grotesque and macabre humor, his use of archaic literary trappings, and the mixture of sacred and profane as points of contact with baroque literature.

———. *A contra prova de Tereza, favo-de-mel*. João Pessoa: Tipografia Chaves, 1973. Treats the structure, the theme of violence and the several sections of *Tereza Batista*.

Brookshaw, David. *Race and Color in Brazilian Literature*. Metuchen, N.J.: Scarecrow Press, 1986. Finds racial stereotyping and prejudice in the characterization of blacks in *Jubiabá*, *Gabriela*, and *Tenda*.

Bruno, Haroldo. "Coroamento do popular." In *Estudos de literatura brasileira*. 2d ser., 237–41. Rio de Janeiro: Leitura, 1966. Sees in *Os velhos marinheiros* a continuation—albeit in the picaresque mode—of the novelist's identification with the common Brazilian, placing him in the tradition of Alencar rather than that of Machado de Assis, which the essayist considers to be elitist.

———. "O sentido da terra na obra de Jorge Amado." In *Estudos de literatura brasileira*. Rio de Janeiro: O Cruzeiro, 1957; rpt. in *Jorge Amado, povo e terra: 40 anos de literatura*, 145–57. São Paulo: Martins, 1972. Article praises telluric quality of Amado's fiction, comparing his novels with those of Lins do Rego.

Cândido [de Mello e Souza], Antônio. "Poesia, documento e história," In *Brigada ligeira.* São Paulo: Martins, 1945; rpt. in *Jorge Amado: 30 anos de literatura,* 168–79. São Paulo: Martins, 1961; rpt. in *Jorge Amado, povo e terra: 40 anos de literatura,* 109–23. São Paulo: Martins, 1972. A balanced, insightful discussion of Amado's early works through *Terras do sem fim.*

Cavalcante, Rodolfo Coelho. *Tereza Batista cansada de guerra.* Folheto autorisado [*sic*] pelo escritor Jorge Amado. Salvador, 1973. A *cordel* poem based on Amado's *Tereza Batista.*

Chamberlain, Bobby J. "Salvador, Bahia, and the Passion According to Jorge Amado." In *The City in the Latin American Novel.* Edited by Bobby J. Chamberlain, 69–82. East Lansing: Latin American Studies Center, Michigan State University, 1980. Outlines the case for regarding *Quincas* as a "pastiche" of the Passion of Christ, noting the author's use of the processes of displacement and condensation.

Costa, Lígia Militz da. *O condicionamento telúrico-ideológico do desejo em "Terras do sem fim" de Jorge Amado.* Porto Alegre: Movimento-Instituto Estadual do Livro, 1976. One of the most useful academic studies of *Terras.*

Curran, Mark J. *Jorge Amado e a literatura de cordel.* Salvador: Fundação Cultural do Estado da Bahia, 1981. Examines the novelist's appropriation of the trappings of *literatura de cordel* in *Pastores, Tenda,* and *Tereza Batista.*

Da Matta, Roberto. "*Dona Flor e seus dois maridos:* Um romance relacional," *Tempo brasileiro 74: Jorge Amado, Km 70* (July-September, 1983):3–33. Applies Bakhtin's concepts of carnivalization and dialogization to *Dona Flor* and other latter-day Amadian works. Sees *Dona Flor* as being based on a "relational model," which he regards as emblematic of Brazilian society.

Dicionário crítico do moderno romance brasileiro, 24–37. Belo Horizonte: Grupo Gente Nova, 1970. A critical discussion of Amado's novels through *Tenda dos milagres* (1969).

Ellison, Fred P. *Brazil's New Novel: Four Northeastern Masters,* 83–108. Berkeley: University of California Press, 1954. Examines various features of Amado's fiction through *Seara vermelha.* One of the earliest studies of the novelist's works in English.

Foster, David W., and Virginia Ramos Foster. *Modern Latin American Literature.* 2 vols. New York: Ungar, 1975. Includes (1, 30–42) excerpts in English translation of fifteen critical essays on Amado's fiction through 1969.

Galvão, Walnice Nogueira. "Amado: Respeitoso, respeitável." In *Saco de gatos: ensaios críticos,* 13–22. São Paulo: Duas Cidades, 1976. A scathing denunciation of *Tereza Batista cansada de guerra.* Labels the protagonist as a unidimensional sexist stereotype, "the ideal woman of progressive men with money in their wallets." Feels the novelist is more interested in titillating the reader than in depicting the prostitute realistically. Alleges author's populism represents an "idealization of poverty" and criticizes him for use of such devices as indirect free style and deus ex machina. Feels that Amado and Érico Veríssimo, who, due to their independence from government jobs, were the most vocal opponents of censorship in 1973, were paradoxically the most dependent on popular literary tastes.

Gattai, Zélia. *Um chapéu para viagem.* Rio de Janeiro: Record, 1983. A memoir of the early years of her marriage to the author, containing an abundance of revealing accounts of their experiences together.

Jorge Amado: Documentos. Lisbon: Europa-América, 1964. Various materials about the author and his works. Includes photographs.

Jorge Amado: Ensaios sobre o escritor. Salvador: Universidade Federal da Bahia, 1982. A collection of essays about various Amadian novels, published on the occasion of the author's seventieth birthday. Includes articles by Eduardo Portella, Afrânio Coutinho, Cláudio Veiga, João Carlos Teixeira Gomes, David Salles, Judith Grossman, Ildázio Tavares, João Eurico Matta, John P. Dwyer, and Hildegardes Vianna.

Jorge Amado, povo e terra: 40 anos de literatura. São Paulo: Martins, 1972. A collection of essays on the novelist's works commemorating the fortieth anniversary of *O país do carnaval.* Includes fifteen essays (emphasizing the recent period), a chronology, Amado's inaugural speech at the Brazilian Academy of Letters, and a letter written by the novelist in response to questions from a reader. Bibliography and photographs.

Jorge Amado: 30 anos de literatura. São Paulo: Martins, 1961. Contains numerous reviews and essays (some in their entirety, others excerpted) on Amado's works from 1931 through 1961. Also includes a chronology, a bibliography, and a photographic history of the author. The volume commemorates Amado's thirtieth anniversary as a published writer.

Jornal de letras, 207 (July 1967). The entire issue is devoted to articles about the novelist and his works.

Lima, Luís Costa. "Jorge Amado," In *A literatura no Brasil.* Edited by Afrânio Coutinho. 2d ed. 6 vols., vol. 5 (Modernismo), 304–26. Rio de Janeiro: Sul Americana, 1970. A largely unsympathetic appraisal of the novelist's fiction through *Pastores.* Regards *Terras do sem fim* as a masterpiece unequaled by subsequent works, which, though possessing notable qualities, serve to point up Amado's limits as a fictionist.

Lowe, Elizabeth. *The City in Brazilian Literature.* Rutherford, N.J.: Fairleigh Dickinson University Press, 1982. Characterizes Amado's depiction of Salvador, Bahia, as "picturesque exoticism," his portrayal of urban poor as "carnivalization."

Lucas, Fábio. "Plano, com epígrafe, de um estudo sobre a morte de Quincas Berro D'água," In *Jorge Amado, povo e terra: 40 anos de literatura,* 179–82. São Paulo: Martins, 1972. A brief but useful article enumerating the mainstays and traditional defects of Amado's fiction as well as the innovations of *Gabriela* and *Quincas.*

Marotti, Giorgio. *Il negro nel romanzo brasiliano.* Roma: Bulzoni, 1982. Chapter 15 (388–461) treats Amado's characterization of blacks in his fiction, which Marotti deems positive in contrast to the racial stereotyping he detects in the works of all earlier Brazilian writers.

————. *Profilo sociologico della letteratura brasiliana Vol. 2, Jorge Amado, brasilidade negra.* Roma: Bulzoni, 1972. Focuses on the question of the author's depiction of Brazilian society, particularly such groups as the poor and blacks.

Martins, Wilson. "A comédia baiana." In *Jorge Amado, povo e terra: 40 anos de literatura,* 165–75. São Paulo: Martins, 1972. A critical analysis of *Dona Flor* and *Tenda,* which the essayist considers as belonging to the novelist's second, mature phase—the *ciclo da comédia baiana*—begun in 1958 with *Gabriela.*

Moraes, Lygia Marina. *Conheça o escritor brasileiro Jorge Amado.* Rio de Janeiro: Record, 1977. Includes excerpts from the novelist's fiction and critical commentary.

Olinto, Antônio. "Os pastores da noite." In *A verdade da ficção: Crítica de romance,* 52–55. Rio de Janeiro: Artes Gráficas, 1966. Examines generic affiliations of the three parts of *Pastores.*

Patai, Daphne. *Myth and Ideology in Contemporary Brazilian Fiction.* Rutherford, N.J.: Fairleigh Dickinson University Press, 1983. Chapter 5 (111–40) is a critique of *Tereza Batista cansada de guerra,* which Patai feels undercuts itself ideologically. Criticizes Amado for his use of the supernatural, for his employment of humor that has the effect of trivializing social injustice, and for what she regards as his patronizing view of the "noble poor." Alleges he panders to base human instincts.

Pescatello, Ann. "The Brazileira: Images and Realities in Writings of Machado de Assis and Jorge Amado," In *Female and Male in Latin America: Essays.* Edited by Ann Pescatello, 29–58. Pittsburgh: University of Pittsburgh Press, 1973. Compares and contrasts Amado's female characters of *Terras, Gabriela, Os velhos marinheiros, Pastores,* and *Dona Flor* with those of Machado de Assis. Detects a preoccupation with class and race in both writers' female characterizations. If such literature is an accurate reflection of the role alternatives available to women in the societies chronicled, then there appears to have been a modicum of progress in the years separating the two authors' fictional worlds.

Portella, Eduardo. "A fábula em cinco tempos," In *Jorge Amado: 30 anos de literatura,* 13–26. São Paulo: Martins, 1961; rpt. in Portella, Eduardo. *Dimensões III,* 105–27. Rio de Janeiro: Tempo Brasileiro, 1965; rpt. in *Jorge Amado, povo e terra: 40 anos de literatura,* 71–84. São Paulo: Martins, 1972. Divides the novelist's works (through *Os velhos marinheiros*) into five distinct periods.

Queiroz Júnior, Teófilo de. *Preconceito de cor e a mulata brasileira.* São Paulo: Ática, 1975. Criticizes novelist's portrayal of Gabriela and Ana Mercedes (*Tenda*) as racist stereotyping.

Rabassa, Gregory. *O negro na ficção brasileira: Meio século de história literária.*

Translated by Ana Maria Martins. Rio de Janeiro: Tempo Brasileiro, 1965. In chapter 7 (263–321), the author details Amado's portrayal of blacks in his fiction through *Seara vermelha* (1946).

Rocha, Hildon. "Revisão de Jorge Amado," In *Entre lógicos e místicos*, 15–29. Rio de Janeiro: São José, 1968. Written in 1958, the article views *Gabriela, cravo e canela* as a turning point not only in Amado's fiction but also in his thinking. Notes his new, nonjudgmental attitude toward characters and his use of irony and humor.

Salema, Álvaro. *Jorge Amado: O homem e a obra; Presença em Portugal*. Lisbon: Europa-América, 1982. Traces Amado's literary development and documents his ties to Portugal. Includes useful photographs.

Sant'Anna, Affonso Romano de. "De como e porque Jorge Amado em *A morte e a morte de Quincas Berro D'água* é um autor carnavalizador, mesmo sem nunca ter-se preocupado com isso," *Tempo brasileiro 74: Jorge Amado, Km 70* (July–September 1983):45–65. Analyzes *Quincas* as an example of Bakhtinian carnivalization.

Santiago, Silviano. "O teorema de Walnice e a sua recíproca," In *Vale quanto pesa*, 69–88. Rio de Janeiro: Paz e Terra, 1982. Concurs with most of Galvão's arguments about *Tereza* and about Amado's alleged subservience to the tastes of the literary marketplace. He goes on to pose the question of whether Brazilian intellectuals of the 1980s and beyond will feel the need, then, to become more dependent on the state (and thus less outspoken politically) in order to free themselves from the tyranny of the "culture industry."

Silverman, Malcolm. "Algumas observações sobre as personagens de Jorge Amado," In *Moderna ficção brasileira: Ensaios*. Trans. by João Guilherme Linke, 137–57. Rio de Janeiro: Civilização Brasileira, 1978. A discussion of the "fifteen novels and one novelette" that begin with *O país do carnaval* (1931) and continue through *Tenda dos milagres* (1969). Divides works into two phases, the second beginning with *Gabriela* (1958).

Slater, Candace. *Stories on a String: The Brazilian Literatura de Cordel*. Berkeley and Los Angeles: University of California Press, 1982. In Chapter 6 (141–63), compares and contrasts the character Tereza Batista in the poem of Rodolfo Coelho Cavalcante with the Amadian original.

Táti, Miécio. "Estilo e revolução no romance de Jorge Amado." In *Jorge Amado, povo e terra: 40 anos de literatura*, 125–43. São Paulo: Martins, 1972. Written in 1951, the essay discusses the novelist's juxtaposition of crude description and lyricism in the novels through *Seara vermelha* (1946).

———. *Jorge Amado: Vida e obra*. Belo Horizonte: Itatiaia, 1960. The first book-length study of the novelist and his works. Contains biographical information as well as plot summaries of and criticial reaction to the author's works through *Quincas* (originally published in 1959).

Tavares, Paulo. *O baiano Jorge Amado e sua obra*. Rio de Janeiro: Record, 1980. Contains a chronology and a bibliography of primary and secondary sources. Includes plot summaries and descriptions of each work. A wealth of information on such things as translations of the author's books, adaptations of them (theater, motion pictures, radio and television dramas, comic books, popular songs, etc.) and the articles, dissertations, and theses that they have generated. Also includes a list of Amado's honors and literary prizes and some photographs.

————. *Criaturas de Jorge Amado.* 2d ed. Rio de Janeiro: Record; Brasília: Instituto Nacional do Livro, 1985. A dictionary of Amado's literary characters through 1979 (*Farda, fardão, camisola de dormir*). Includes a useful list of real people who have appeared in the author's fiction. The first edition (São Paulo: Martins, 1969) lists characters through *Dona Flor* (1966).

Tempo brasileiro 74: Jorge Amado, Km 70 (July–September 1983). A collection of recent essays on various Amadian novels from Roberto Da Matta, Maria do Carmo P. Pandolfo, Affonso Romano de Sant'Anna, Ilana Strozemberg, Luciana Stegagno Picchio, Vera Figueiredo, and Eduardo Portella.

Articles

Baden, Nancy Tucker. "Popular Poetry in the Novels of Jorge Amado." *Journal of Latin American Lore* 2.1 (Summer 1976): 3–22. Analyzes the novelist's inclusion of ABCs, religious songs, work songs, children's songs, etc., in his fiction.

————. "The Significance of Names in Jorge Amado's *Gabriela, cravo e canela*," *Proceedings of the Pacific Coast Council on Latin American Studies* 3 (1974): 87–94. Examines symbolism of characters' names, names as a reflection of social class, and irony as it relates to the novelist's use of names.

Bernard, Judith. "Narrative Focus in Jorge Amado's Story of Vasco Moscoso de Aragão." *Romance Notes* 3.1 (Autumn 1966): 14–17. Discusses the role of the "picaresque" narrator in *Comandante,* alleging that Amado's "inconsistent use of this point of view" mars the narrative framework.

Chamberlain, Bobby J. "Deus, deuses e *deus ex machina* n'*Os lusíadas* e na ficção contemporânea de Jorge Amado," *Hispania* 68 (1985):716–23. Explores the use of the supernatural in Camões's epic and in several recent Amadian novels. Attaches a satirical and compensatory function to Amado's inclusion of Afro-Brazilian divinities.

————. "Double Perspective in Two Works of Jorge Amado," *Estudos iberoamericanos* 4.1 (July 1978): 81–88. Compares and contrasts the novelist's use of double perspective in *Quincas* and *Comandante.*

————. "Gastronomic Interludes in Jorge Amado's *Dona Flor e seus dois maridos,*" *Tropos* 6.1 (Spring 1977): 19–26. A discussion of the author's use of introductory recipes and menus and their integration into the novel's structure.

————. "Unlocking the *Roman à Clef:* A Look at the 'In-Group' Humor of Jorge Amado," *American Hispanist* 4.28 (September 1978): 12–16. Analyzes the processes that Amado uses in incorporating real people into the fictional universe.

Corominas, Juan M. "Incidencia femenina en la estructura de *Gabriela, cravo e canela,*" *Hispania* 68 (1985): 484–89. A description of the author's use of female characters to structure the novel.

Dantas, Paulo. "Os caminhos de Jorge Amado," *Revista brasiliense* 37 (1961): 164–71. Laments the disappearance of Amado the revolutionary in *Gabriela* and *Os velhos marinheiros,* detecting in the latter works an excessive dose of picaresque humor.

Ellison, Fred P. "Social Symbols in Some Recent Brazilian Literature." *The Texas Quarterly* 3.3 (Autumn 1960): 112–26. Analyzes the presence of "social symbols" such as the bandit, the drought refugee, and the religious fanatic in Rachel de Queiroz's *A beata Maria do Egito,* Amado's *Gabriela,* and the memoirs of José Lins do Rego and Graciliano Ramos.

Fitz, Earl E. "Structural Ambiguity in Jorge Amado's *A morte e a morte de Quincas Berro D'água,*" *Hispania* 67 (1984): 221–28. Analyzes the author's use of deliberate ambiguity in the narration of *Quincas.*

Furter, Pierre. "Do valor atual da teoria lukacsiana." *Tempo Brasileiro* 2.3 (March 1963): 134–55. *Gabriela* and *Os velhos marinheiros* are given as examples of Lukács's concept of "critical realism."

Hamilton, Russell G. "Afro-Brazilian Cults in the Novels of Jorge Amado," *Hispania* 50 (1967): 242–52. Documents the author's treatment of *macumba* and *candomblé* through *Os pastores da noite.*

"Jorge, descansado de guerra." Review of *Tereza Batista cansada de guerra, Visão,* 15 January 1973, 69–70. Unsigned review-article. Assails Amado's populism and alleged preference for the picturesque, charging that he romanticizes poverty, backwardness, and ignorance while proffering a simplistic, Manichean view of the world.

Lowe, Elizabeth Schlomann. "The 'New' Jorge Amado," *Luso-Brazilian Review* 6.2 (December 1969): 73–82. Analyzes the "new Amado" in *Gabriela, Quincas,* and *Dona Flor,* contending that humor is the key to the author's change in style. Detects in *Quincas* a "bizarre parallel with the death and resurrection of Christ."

Mazzara, Richard A. "Poetry and Progress in Jorge Amado's *Gabriela, cravo e canela,*" *Hispania* 46 (1963): 551–56. An analysis of the four heroines of *Gabriela*—Ofenísia, Glória, Malvina, and Gabriela—and their relationship to the novel's introductory poems. Touches on the topic of changing sex roles.

Noblat, Ricardo. "Os personagens vivos de Jorge Amado," *Manchete,* 3 March 1973, 42–49. Contains information on several of the novelist's real-life characters, along with Amado's and Noblat's observations regarding the process of incorporating real persons into fictional characterizations.

Nunes, Maria Luisa. "The Preservation of African Culture in Brazilian Literature: The Novels of Jorge Amado," *Luso-Brazilian Review* 10 (1973): 86–101. An examination of Amado's portrayal of African culture in *Jubiabá, Mar morto, Capitães da areia, Os pastores da noite,* and *Tenda dos milagres.* Concludes that the novelist's works are among the most important vehicles for preserving African culture in Brazil.

Rabassa, Gregory. "The Five Faces of Love in Jorge Amado's Bahian Novels," *Revista de letras* 4 (1963): 94–103. Detects five categories of love present in *Jubiabá, Mar morto,* and *Capitães da areia,* associating each with one of the identities of the Afro-Brazilian goddess, Iemanjá.

Schade, George D. "Three Contemporary Brazilian Novels: Some Comparisons and Contrasts," *Hispania* 39 (1956): 391–96. Considers *Terras do sem fim* to be inferior to Ramos's *Angústia* and Queiroz's *As três Marias* with regard to the quality of the writing and the writers' probing of the characters' minds.

Silverman, Malcolm. "Allegory in Two Works of Jorge Amado," *Romance Notes* 13.1 (Autumn 1971): 67–70. Detects in *Jubiabá* the motif of the chivalric romance and in *Pastores* an allegory of the Passion of Christ.

————. "Moral Dilemma in Jorge Amado's *Dona Flor e seus dois maridos*," *Romance Notes* 13.2 (Winter 1971): 243–49. Traces Dona Flor's emotional and psychological trajectory toward ultimate compromise.

Vincent, Jon S. "Jorge Amado, Jorge desprezado." *Luso-Brazilian Review* 15, Supplementary Issue (Summer 1978): 11–17. An examination of the reasons for which readers enjoy the works of Amado. Includes a critique of Galvão's contention that Tereza Batista is an unrealistic portrayal of the prostitute.

Unpublished Dissertations and Theses

Baden, Nancy Tucker. "Jorge Amado: Storyteller of Bahia (A Study of Narrative Technique)." Ph.D. Diss., University of California, Los Angeles, 1971.

Chamberlain, Bobby J. "Humor: Vehicle for Social Commentary in the Novels of Jorge Amado." Ph.D. Diss., University of California, Los Angeles, 1975.

Silverman, Malcolm. "An Examination of the Characters in Jorge Amado's *Ciclo da comédia baiana*." Ph.D. Diss., University of Illinois, Urbana-Champaign, 1971.

Turner, Doris Jean. "The Poor and Social Symbolism: An Examination of Three Novels of Jorge Amado." Ph.D. Diss., St. Louis University, 1967.

Vincent, Jon S. "Jorge Amado: Politics and the Novel." Ph.D. Diss., University of New Mexico, 1970.

Index